5 Steps to B d

From Mopping Floors to Making Millions on Instagram

RONNE BROWN

A POST HILL PRESS BOOK
ISBN: 978-1-68261-536-2
ISBN (eBook): 978-1-68261-537-9

From Mopping Floors to Making Millions on Instagram:
5 Steps to Building an Online Brand

Cover art by Dan Pitts

Post Hill Press
New York • Nashville
posthillpress.com

Published in the United States of America

DEDICATION

To my children Damari, Amor, Marvin, and Rio.

Growing up, I was taught to live a cookie-cutter life. Success meant work like everyone else, think like everyone else, and live like everyone else.

As I've grown, my outlook on life and success has changed. I've sketched out what success will look like for me and made it my reality. I want you to know that you have the power to do the same. Your wildest dreams, craziest visions, or weirdest concepts can come to life and change the entire world. You have the power of the internet at your fingertips! Use it to create a life and business that revolve around your schedule, your interest, your happiness, and your passion no matter how crazy it may appear to be to others. Risk being misunderstood and go for it! Trust me.

CONTENTS

PREFACE

I grew up in a beautiful family, unfortunately as time progressed the fussing and disagreements between my parents turned into a broken marriage. My mom left. Then my dad's mom died, and he took a hard hit. Things went sour fast. He went through a very dark depression and was looking for companionship in the wrong places and from the wrong women—young women who were addicted to drugs and just wanted to use him for his money. They started to bring drugs into the home and inviting other drug addicts into the home while my dad was at work. I can never imagine what it must have been like for my dad to lose his wife *and* his mom *and* his job within an eighteen-month span. I don't judge and I love my father to this day. The impact on me was that I became a teen mom at sixteen years old. By the time I was twenty-three, I had already been counted out. Now, my income averages roughly seven figures a year. My monthly salary exceeds what I used to make in an entire year. I have a savings account balance in the six figures. To me, six figures in a bank account is the new sexy. But I didn't become successful overnight.

My story is for you if you are in the seed-planting phase of your life. I want you to understand there's a process that goes with success. Although I am highly successful now, many people didn't see all the hardships I endured. Hardships such as figuring out how to feed my family while still smiling. Wondering all the time, "How am I going to do this?" If you take nothing else away from this book, I want you to know it didn't take just one year of hard work to achieve my success, it took close to a decade and I am still building it. I struggled with doubt often, and sometimes felt as if, maybe, I should give up because success wasn't happening as fast as I wanted. I can't tell you how many times I thought, "I should find a regular job," even though I knew my calling was to teach and mentor other people and get them to the point where they took action.

I want you to know you are not alone in this journey. There are other people in the world who have gone through similar challenges. I also want you to know that perfection doesn't exist. I will share with you my own journey from growing up in a crack house and being a teen mom, to earning a seven-figure annual salary. I want you to see that sharing your story, your journey, your truth with others is the key to connection and influence. By not "faking it 'til you make it" or covering up your story or being embarrassed by your circumstances, you can be free. For me, transparency is what has motivated other people to take action and really change their game.

This book is for the woman who has come to a time and place in her life where she is tired of settling, whether it's business, whether it's lack of compensation, or whether it's dimming her light when she knows she should shine. It could be all of those things. You may be reading this book because you feel like you've been counted out, or you're afraid to take a leap on something. You feel like you are running out of time. You feel like if you don't do it now—whatever "it" is for you—you will never really get around to it, and you need that last bit of inspiration that's going to encourage you to take action. You have been empowered but you need the thing that's going to make you move. Maybe you are at the implementation phase of going after it and this book is exactly what you've been looking for.

My biggest goal with this book is to provide you with real tools to get you to a place where you will create results in your life. I have spent five years leading over 30,000 people, teaching them how to sell, how to brand themselves online, and how to earn a six-figure income. And now, I am going to teach you, too. If you have been passed over, marginalized, ignored, if you feel like your earnings don't reflect your self-worth, read on.

Introduction:

Women Are the Future

I never used to be open and honest about my past. As a woman especially, when we walk into a room, we have our armor on. Ready, made up, game face on. Instantly looking one another up and down, picking one another apart. I started to think about how people would receive me when I would walk into a room trying to fake it. Super confident, "my-life-is-perfect, I-don't-need-to-share-my-lows, and my-personal-business-is-my-personal-business" attitude. When I walked into a room as that person, I didn't get much of a response. But just think. Wouldn't you like to meet a woman who walks into a room and says, "Hey, I'm Ronne. Here's a little bit about me. I had three kids before I was twenty-five. I grew up in a very rough atmosphere. I struggled with knowing my standards in my dating life. I love having a good time. I love dancing. I appreciate my friendships." When I came in like that, women automatically let their guard down, accepted me, and counted me in.

If we led with all of our crap versus all of the crap we have, people would accept us so much more. I used to be embarrassed to share my story. I was embarrassed about having three kids at such a young age. I remember working and people asking me, "How many kids do you have?" I would reply, "I've got kids." I didn't even want to say I had three kids. So many people have made fun of me, judged me when I was already ashamed of being a mom. I used to be ashamed of that. I used to be ashamed for having a relationship that didn't work out with my kids' dad. I used to be ashamed for getting fired. I used to be ashamed for not going to college. I used to be ashamed for having to admit that I was evicted from my apartment as a kid. Shame is not shameful. Being ashamed is shameful. Society judges and we judge ourselves based on the judgement of others who shouldn't matter.

Anything is possible right now for women. Years ago, if we went into a meeting, we had to be dressed a certain way. We would have to wear long skirts that weren't revealing. Basically, we had to act like men or at the very least, never reveal that we were women. *Never let them see you cry! Don't show weakness.* This was the mantra of a woman working in a man's world. Now, we are shattering glass ceilings. We have the power to bring our spunk into whatever the hell we want.

If we want to show up for a boardroom meeting wearing a freaking black leather jacket with studs, we can. If we want to dye our hair blue, we can. It's no longer a reflection or representation of us being unprofessional, it is more about expressing our personality.

Now, anything is possible. We can turn our hobbies into profit. If you like being a comedian all day and telling jokes, you can leverage that. If you like being a surfer, that can be a business. If you like sitting on the couch eating different hot dogs, there's someone who will pay you to hear your review on the different brands. I promise you, there is a way to leverage whatever you love, and this is the time where we can benefit from doing the things that we actually enjoy rather than doing what people used to tell us we *had* to do to make a living.

In the next ten years, I see various influences dominating people with opinions they aren't afraid to share, leading the conference meetings and the boardroom discussions. I see innovation. I see the risk-takers leading the way. I see the people who aren't afraid to do the things that are normal and I see abnormal becoming cool again. I see the rule breakers leading the pack. I see women rising to the top. I just see a future of art, innovation, the weird $&@# being cool, and the stupidest things thriving in the market. I see the craziest jobs evolving. I see people wanting more freedom in every aspect, where no one is sitting in a boardroom anymore and everyone works from home. *That's* what I see.

I see women having higher standards because they are now creating the six-figure incomes that corporate America won't give them. Women are now saying what they will and will not accept. They are now turning down marriages because they are busy building their companies. They're bringing their children with them to the office. They are teaching their daughters not to settle and showing them to be someone instead of somebody's, not to be defined by the men they're with. They are showing them they don't have to be afraid to walk away. Women used to be controlled by the person they were with, and if they were single they felt like they had no worth. Now, if you're single, it's because you choose to be and often because you are not settling or investing time unless it's to a certain standard. Women, thank goodness, are finally starting to realize "I'm the win." Women are now looking for men who have something to bring to the table. *Women are bringing the table.*

Taught to Be the Help, Not Lead the Help

I want to show the little brown girls who look like me that they can have it all if that's what they want. In May 2017, I gave the commencement speech at HD Woodson High School. After I left, the biggest thing I said that resonated with me was that, growing up there were no successful black women for me to look up to, or meet in person, or even know personally. Sure, there were people in Hollywood and Oprah Winfrey, but they didn't live in my neighborhood. I already had it set in my mind that I would never *ever* freaking meet or see these people.

There was not one person I could talk to who had ever been successful, or lived in their dream home, or had a pool in the backyard, or ever had financial freedom. There was no one to show me that you could sit home and work for yourself. Nobody ever told me you could be a CEO. Everyone always said, "Oh yeah, girl, go to college and go work for someone else."

When you're raised to be the help versus being raised to lead the help, you're taught that you are going to work for someone else, especially if you are a young black woman. No one really talks to you about all the dreams to reach for. In my whole life, no one ever told me, "You can be the boss. You can have your own company." Your parents literally motivate you to go to school, go to college, and convince someone else to employ you.

The crazy thing is, even if you were to ever talk about doing something like that, where I come from, people put you down for dreaming big. *Look at you*, they would say. *Let me pull that air out of your head really quick.* Or, *you're kidding, right?* Or, *who the hell do you think you are?* Or, *you don't realize that it's not possible?* I heard it all growing up. *Shut up, you can't do that.*

I learned later that this is known as the crab mentality, sometimes referred to as "crabs in the bucket." It is a way of thinking best described by the phrase, "If I can't have it, neither can you." The metaphor refers to a bucket of crabs. Individually, the crabs could easily escape from the bucket, but instead, collectively, they grab at one another, which prevents any from escaping and ensures none get out. They all stay at the bottom of the bucket together.

Our parents were brought up in fear and extended that fear to the next generation. I remember when I told my mom I was starting my business and that I was going to quit my job. She said, "Are you crazy? Are you really going to do something like that? Are you going to go sell stuff? You're nuts, right?" At that time, I had three kids. She said, "You have three children. What are you thinking?"

At first, I was angry at her for not being encouraging, for not believing and supporting me and telling me to go for it. But then it was like God communicated to me and He said, "Pause. Think. She was brought up to think like that. It's not that she doesn't believe in you, it is what she was taught. She was brought up in fear. She was brought up not to have dreams. Your ancestors were brought up working for other people and always being taught to be the worker and someone else paying them. It's a generational thing. It's not your mom not believing in you."

Once my mom saw it was possible, her attitude changed. "Oh, my daughter is a rock star," and "Oh my gosh, you can be an entrepreneur now." Now she's ecstatic about my business and passes out my cards and my fliers. She believes in entrepreneurship, but she wasn't able to believe in it before; no one had shown her it was possible. She had a lack of education in that area.

The Midlife Crisis

I have noticed there are three pivotal ages: twenty-five, thirty-five, and sixty. I call them my midlife crises. When you're twenty-five, you are trying to figure out what the hell you are supposed to be doing. What is my mission here?

At thirty-five, you're thinking, "Okay. I thought that was my mission, and now it's time for me to really do what I want to do because I was doing whatever at twenty-five, just to get paid." And I really have to make this happen. That's when implementation kicks in. The implementation phase, because you're $&@#-scared that you are already past thirty and haven't figured out what you're supposed to do yet.

And then there's, sixty. You're at the "sorry, but I'm not going out like that" phase. You have faked it for the last twenty years because you were afraid; you stayed with a man who wanted you to be average, and you wanted to be a wife. Now, you're at a place where you feel like, you know what, "Screw that." You begin to tell yourself, "I am really going to focus on that passion before they put me in the ground."

If you find yourself at one of these ages, the best thing you can do is prepare for that time in your life. People are more relaxed when they have a target or goal they are working towards. When you're strategizing and you have a plan in place, you always feel like you are working towards something. The best thing you can do is write out your timeline:

- Where do you want to be by the time you are twenty-five, thirty-five, and sixty years old? What would you like to accomplish by these ages?
- What do you want your savings account to look like, your retirement account, and your estate? What do you want to have already acquired by these three ages?

Have a plan in front of you because people mostly break down because they don't have a plan. When you have a strategy in front of you, you will increase your chances of avoiding a breakdown or existential crisis because you are clearly working towards something that matters to you.

Part One

Chapter One:

How I Became an Entrepreneur

As far back as I can remember, my mom and dad were arguing a lot. Their marriage was definitely going south, and my mom got to a place in her thinking where she felt like she deserved more. Even at this place in her life, I was her advocate for going after more and making it happen, and she finally acquired the confidence to do it. I was shocked because she had threatened to leave a few times before then, but she never did. My grandfather would come down from New Jersey and pack up her bags, and she would come right back. But this time, she did it. She left and stayed away.

After that I stayed with my father. At that point of my life, my dad could do no wrong in my eyes. I didn't know what the expectations were when it came to having a husband, so I didn't understand my mom's frustration. I loved her enough to see that she wasn't happy, and I encouraged her to move.

The more I lived with my father and the older I got, the more I began to see his imperfections because I wasn't an innocent little girl anymore. I was a teenager and I had a boyfriend. I started to notice the inconsistency of my dad, the women in his life, and his lifestyle.

The next thing I knew, my grandma passed away, and I was pregnant with my son. My grandma was so disappointed in me for getting pregnant (which is something I never really shared with the public), and her lack of support and being embarrassed by me hurt. I thought she would be more supportive. We were mad at each other when she passed away. We never really got to make up. It was basically about me being pregnant and nothing else factored into our relationship. It was a sad ending to a close relationship that should have held more meaning.

Although I had been encouraged to terminate my pregnancy, I didn't. I hid my pregnancy in school. My biggest goal was to show them all that just because I had a child, that didn't mean my life was over. I could still be successful. So I had my son.

I started working. I even tried going to college. After six months, with a small baby to care for, it was overwhelming. The course load required more attention than my baby and I couldn't, *wouldn't*, make that sacrifice. Besides, I needed to focus on creating income as fast as possible because things were going downhill. My dad had gone through a deep depression when his mom died. He was looking for love and it led him to start looking for it in all the wrong places. He had younger women who were on drugs who wanted to date him. Although he thought they really liked him, they just wanted his money.

It got to the point that our rent payments were late, women were moving into our house, and they were stealing my clothes and anything else they could get their paws on. The atmosphere in the house from the women on drugs, who were also bringing in other people who were on drugs when my dad was at work, was my biggest motivation to get the hell out of there.

By the time I was eighteen, I applied for my first apartment and I went to work. I worked as a janitor in a hospital. By nineteen, I'd had my second child. I was mopping floors and doing all the jobs being a janitor entailed—while I was pregnant. A *pregnant janitor* at Georgetown University Hospital. I went from there into entrepreneurship.

In my short life, I've worked as a janitor, a travel agent, a bank teller, an assistant in a copy center, a contract manager for a college, a paralegal, and a sales assistant at a GAP store. I worked for a telephone company as an analyst, making sure everyone was getting charged a consistent rate across the board. I started my own cleaning company. I was working in the federal government as an acquisitions specialist. I was a "Jill" of all trades but I had no specialty.

I realized how difficult it was for women, especially mothers, to thrive in corporate America. A six-week maternity leave is just not enough time to spend with your baby; mothering doesn't end after six weeks. That's what people don't talk about. They never discuss doctor appointments. No one talks about school activities. They don't talk about the mommy-and-daughter brunches you miss, or that your children look like they have a parent who doesn't care. You ask your supervisor about attending and they don't let you go because they don't care. They are invested in *their* business, not *your* family.

No one ever tells you that when one child becomes ill, the whole house does. That happens multiple times during cold season, and your employer doesn't care. After one or two times of having a cold that will take the whole house out, you get fired.

For me, going through that process just brings back the lack of equality, not just from a race standpoint, but the lack of equality for women. Where is our support for having to go to the doctors' appointments? Having to be home if one child gets sick? You are the nurturer, the caregiver, the provider. I started getting fired from job after job because I had to take my kids to appointments, to the doctor. When you have multiple children, it's like there is never enough leave for you. Never enough support for you. You end up looking like a worker who doesn't work.

That happened to me often in the work field. I couldn't be there for my kids. I could barely get them to the doctors. So many appointments: one-year-olds shots, three-year-olds shots, this appointment, that appointment. If you don't take them to the all their appointments, they can't go to school. They have to get a yearly physical.

Then something shifted. I ended up in managerial positions; with no freaking training or credibility. My voice in an interview landed me those positions. I walked out of the interview, astounded. I had a job…in a law firm. I didn't have a degree but was now going to be responsible for a staff of twenty-five people. I was twenty-five years old. I was not a college graduate and the people I was managing were in their forties. I realized what it was. It was *me*. I was crazy enough to apply for the position and believe in myself. My confidence shined through in those interviews.

I remember that awful day after the last time I was fired and before I started my business. I was two minutes late for work. At the time the company had some "time management" survey underway where a woman monitored our arrivals. She was a very determined individual.

I arrived two minutes late and was called into the office. It was close to Christmas. She told me they were going to fire me. I had a baby in my belly; I was around eight or nine months pregnant. I didn't know what the hell I was going to do. My tags were expired on my car and I had taken a risk driving to work because I didn't have any money to pay a ticket had I received one.

My boss called me in and told me she was going to let me go; I got down on my knees and begged her to let me stay. On. My. Knees. I now look back at that and wonder what I was thinking. Begging felt like my only option at the time. I told her, "Please. I need this. I have another child at home. I'm working. My second child is coming. I have bills to pay. I'm at a very low place in my life right now." She told me she would let me keep my job.

I worked my butt off that whole day. At the end of my shift, I was called into the office again. They decided to let me go anyway. This was the last time, when I finally said entrepreneurship was going to be my thing, I wanted to start my own business. I will never forget that drive home. I cried the whole way. It was the longest ride home in my life. I got home and had a fake smile on trying to tell my child and unborn baby that everything was going to be okay and mommy would have a little more time to spend with them. Deep down inside I was in panic mode because I didn't have money to pay my rent. I didn't have money to pay my other bills. Then I gave myself the proverbial kick in the butt. No more sobbing. Get up and do something about it.

I decided that I was not going to work for anyone, anymore. I was going out on my own. I looked around my house, where I saw a candles and makeup. The point I want to make is look at what you love to do, what are you always doing, look around your house, and build your business around that.

For me, I wouldn't start a business in the electronics field because I don't like science. But I am confident enough to know that if I operate in my purpose, in my passion, it will conquer any fears that come with it. I'm always confident when it comes to talking beauty and fashion in business because those are the things I enjoy doing. I can talk about those all day. When you're doing something that isn't truly in your heart, you feel like you're working. There's a saying, "Do what you love, and you'll never work a day in your life." It's true.

I decided I was going to make a body and bath line. But I was nearly broke; I just had three hundred bucks to my name. I jumped on Google to look up how to make homemade makeup, mineral-based makeup, and organic candles.

I used half of my three hundred dollars and ordered products from a site that offered them at cost. For example, with one box of soy, I could make fifty to sixty candles that could retail for twenty-five dollars each.

The product arrived within three or four days. I got to work immediately. I read the directions and started producing makeup, mineral-based makeup, and organic candles in my home. I posted on Facebook, and someone asked me if they could buy some of my products. From there, I started making these candles in large quantities. I lined up jars at my house and I melted down the soy and added essentials oils.

I started by making social media pages to promote my products. Then I designed a website. It was a simple, inexpensive plug-and-play website. Remember, I had no money so everything I did had to be free or as close to free as possible. I leveraged what I had, which at the time was my time. I used PayPal buttons on my website. Then I started telling everyone that I was launching my own homemade makeup and candle line. I started posting and sharing the line on Facebook. I started engaging with my Facebook friends, asking, how many of you like candles, and what are your favorite scents? I started asking for feedback *before* I launched a product to try to get potential customers. This is where I began learning what works. It was the start of me building a profitable online profile. Using the strategies that I am now going to teach you in this book, I first got one order. Then five orders a week. Then ten orders a week.

I next started wondering where I could display my products and begin making profits offline. I checked Craigslist, Eventbrite, and other sites to look for local events. I scoured the newspaper. All I had to ask was, "Can I set up a table, please?" I would sell at events every weekend. If I could do an event on Friday, Saturday, and Sunday, I would. I would go to farmers' markets, set my table up, and before I knew it, I was selling—sometimes as much as two hundred dollars' worth of product per event. For a three-hundred-dollar investment in product, I could make one thousand dollars, leaving me a profit of seven hundred dollars. That would be enough for me to pay my rent and order a pizza for my kids.

From there, I started hosting my own events. I saw that women liked events and I started bringing them in, empowering them, and having girl talk before selling my products to them. It just began to grow. That's how so many women started gravitating towards me. Then I thought of another idea and started offering to do their makeup.

I think I fell in love with having a woman come to me who might not feel good about herself, and then seeing her get a makeover or beauty treatment and watching her confidence rise. Sometimes someone would come to me who was very shy, but by the time she left me, she was talking and sharing her life, and we were laughing and feeling like girlfriends.

The relationship building that I had been perfecting in all those jobs started taking off, and it started to make sense. I started to ask people more about themselves to get them talking. I learned that from my job as a janitor. Then the next thing I knew, my makeup line was going and people were reaching out to me to come to their event and set up a table. People would ask me, "Hey. I'm going to have girl's night at my house. Can you come over?"

I went from attending events and doing home parties to taking the next step, and the next risk. I wanted to open a salon. I didn't want just to work in it; I just wanted to *own* it. So I partnered with two young ladies who were stylists, and boy, was *that* a learning experience. I had to learn how to manage people and really own a brick-and-mortar business, which is a whole different ball game.

I created a culture in the salon that was different. Women would come just to sit down and talk to me. I knew they were coming in because they wanted to spend time with me, though they would get their makeup and hair done too. The crazy thing was, the salon was not located in the best area of town, but clients would make the trip anyway. They didn't care. I used to serve them wine as they walked in, and it became a place where they wanted to hang out. The most valuable thing I offered them was *not* the wine, but my ear. These salon clients didn't have many people who would take an interest in their lives. What people don't realize in business is that it's very rare to have someone take the time just to sit and listen to you.

I learned the value of being a good listener and providing feedback. It's really not about the product; it's truly about letting the customer know you care about them. You almost become a counsellor as a business owner when you have customers. This taught me how important relationship building is, and that people really don't care about anything other than how you make them feel.

That's when the direct sales came in and I found out about a certain product, because when you own a salon, people walk in all day. They're trying to sell you stuff, and that product walked into my door. At this point, I'm running a business, making money, and my life has done a 360-degree turnaround. But it's still just like, "hmm, something's missing." What happened was I really didn't have the time to spend with my kids because I became a workaholic. I was catering to other people's needs so much on a Friday or on a Saturday that my children started missing me. I was still working part-time because I had picked up a job in the state government. I was leaving that job and going to the salon and working on the weekends too. I was making money but my kids needed me, they missed me.

I started to research online marketing because when that product came in at first, I didn't know about it. I just knew someone sold you something at a low price and you sell it at a higher price. That was all I knew: show up to get paid, show up to get paid, show up to get paid. Exchange time for money. I didn't understand leveraging. I didn't understand online marketing. I didn't understand automation. As I sat down first with the product and then with people, and did a little more research, I started to post about it online. I realized I didn't have to be at an office to make money.

I am always seeking information; that's my thing. I want to know more and more. I can never have enough information. I started to wonder, how I can continue to get the skin care and wellness products in front of more people to make more money. A lightbulb went off in my mind: the internet. I started to befriend more people online, to engage with more people online. I took every concept I had learned from being a janitor, working at the law firm, and being a travel agent, and started to apply it to my perception of online marketing. Talk with people when they comment on your photos; build relationships with them; respond. I started to apply those things and *that's* when my life started to change. I practiced with all the tools I am going to provide you in this book.

I would wake up and I would already have ten orders. Right now, as I'm writing this book, it's 12:33 and there's an alert on my phone that someone has placed two orders for 138 dollars. I haven't done anything except eat bacon, eggs, and popcorn so far today. Learning automation, learning to leverage, and realizing the future is going to be online. If you don't keep up, you are going to get left behind. When I learned that, that's when my success took off.

Never Lose Sight of What Is Most Important

I was a janitor for two years. I was cleaning up after people, mopping floors, changing sheets, wiping blood (and other bodily functions that don't need to be specified), doing what I had to do to keep my family fed and a roof over our heads.

When I was in that position, I learned how to communicate with people at different levels of their lives, from doctors to "regular" people in the hospital. But the biggest thing I learned was from being able to see rich people on their deathbeds. I watched them not worry about money; everything shifted from money to family and love.

I think God wanted me to see that shift before I got to where I am, so I never lose sight of what is most important in life. Not money. Not success. But family, impacting other people's lives, and love. Those are our greatest achievements. Another realization was that I never saw anyone on their deathbed asking for the tools to make a million dollars.

Another observation: Those rich people were all talking about their kids. The biggest, no, the two biggest things I learned were that family and love will be most important to you, and to never leave this earth with regrets.

When I entered patients' rooms and cleaned up, they would start conversations with me. These people, confined to a bed in a hospital, would talk about all the $&@# they could have done, would have done, and how they should have done it—if they could start over. Now they're sick or they're dying, and they regret how they took their family for granted or how they should have done that dream thing they wanted to do but were afraid.

As I started working hard and I started generating more income, I started dreaming bigger. I was thinking, "That's not my dream home." That was me transitioning from an apartment to a first-time homebuyer. Then I was a first-time homebuyer home. That wasn't my dream home. But it was a next step in getting to our dream.

Family First as an Entrepreneur

You can't allow your "business" to strip you from your ultimate goal. A lot of times, our why is our children. It's our family. It's our husband. It's our mom. It's the people who matter most to us that we're doing it for, right? You're starting a business so you can have more time with *them*. You're starting a business so you can have more freedom. You're starting a business because you want to build an inheritance for them, to give them opportunities that you never had. But what tends to happen to people is that they get so caught up in the game that they forget it's okay to pause, sit back, and enjoy life for a second. If I say that I'm doing this for my kids but I get so caught up in doing it that I'm not spending time with them, then how am I using what I'm working for to benefit them?

You work so hard to be able to relax, to take a vacation, but once you start working you never relax. You never take vacations. You're doing this because you want to be a stay-at-home mom, but once you start your own business, you're working so much that you're never home to *be* a mom. You can't allow a business or its success or the process involved to make you so freaking busy that you can't appreciate the things that truly matter or the people for whom you're really doing it. What good am I to my kids if I'm always gone, if I'm always working, if I'm never home, or if I am home but I'm too busy even to talk to them? There's no point, so we have to realize and understand the importance of balance.

Right now, many business leaders teach that balance doesn't exist. I hear that so often, and that's not true. Balance exists if you make it a priority in your life; I think the biggest thing is knowing where the reward comes from spiritually. We fall into the mistake of thinking that our actions drive success and the harder we work, the more we get, but there's a spiritual connection there as well. My God is the ultimate provider. You may think that success is built 100 percent on work ethic, but it has so much to do with your gratitude, your heart, your energy, and that God knows that if He elevates you, you're going to use it for His glory and His good. He can provide for you.

Here is a prime example. During my first two years of business, I was working my butt off, staying up until 5:00 and 6:00 in the morning. My husband would be coming down for breakfast while I would be going up to bed. I was *so* eager, *so* ambitious, and I wanted success so badly that I tried to rush the process. In actuality, I was a fool on fire. Because you are a fool if you think that you alone are making this happen. If the man above doesn't sign off on it, it's not going to happen for you. If you begin to fall in love with the game, the money, and the success you won't realize the risk to your time with your husband and with your family.

If you don't know your limitations, you will end up lost. I know many successful women right now who are making millions of dollars—but they're divorced. Why? Because they were so tuned in to playing the game, making the money, and being successful, that they stopped lying next to their husbands at night. Their pillow talk faded away. Their romance disappeared. Their friendships were gone because they were more interested in being friends with Benjamin Franklin versus their spouse, whom they'd known for fifteen to twenty years of their life.

You have to decide that you aren't willing to risk it all for money and success. My first two years when I worked my tail off, people would call me at 1:00 or 2:00 in the morning. I had no boundaries in place. I wore myself thin. I would be on conference calls at 1:00 a.m. My husband would be in the bed and I would be on the phone. The light would be on and I would be scrolling through my phone. I had to check myself. My kids started saying things like, "Mom, you're always on the phone. Mom, you're always on the computer." I had to make a change when I realized, I am present but I'm not present. Right?

I made a decision I was going to change. I came up with a schedule and created boundaries in my business. I told people that on Saturdays after 2:00 p.m., I wasn't available. On Sundays now, I don't answer my phone at all. On weekdays, I told people, don't call me after 2:00 p.m. Write your questions on Monday and I will acknowledge every question by Thursday. I started implementing systems and schedules into my business. This was during year three. As I said, during the first two years I let it go unchecked, and it ran me crazy.

Well, guess what happened? During year three, I made more money than I had in year one. How is that possible? Because I was running myself ragged those first two years, I was not getting quiet time. I was not putting myself in a place where I forced other people to think or where I took time for me to focus on self-care. When I implemented boundaries, people started to respect me more as a leader. They valued my time more and my business started to grow. I think my income increased two hundred thousand dollars in the span of one year. Mind-blowing.

In year three, when I was at work I focused solely on income-producing activities versus the years when I was running myself thin. Then I was doing everything and anything just to be busy. Sometimes when you're working like that, you're so busy that you're busy *looking* busy—but you're not really busy doing income-producing things. I now see the difference after I made the adjustments and started working on a schedule. There was a difference, even when it was just my husband and I being able to sit up and talk at night and laugh with each other, joking and talking about our goals and our future.

Now my phone doesn't ring as much. My phone used to ring every hour on the minute. Literally, I would get about three calls an hour, because I started to say, "Yes, yes, yes, yes, yes," to everything. I was desperate for success. Once I started to turn the phone off and implement a schedule, I started to say, "No, no, no, no, no" to others. Once I said "Yes" to my own sanity, my business started to evolve.

I also started to implement automation, which changed my game. I implemented a schedule and stuck to it; there was no bending it. I batched work. When it came to my social media posts, I prepped Monday through Sunday posts. I had them already ready and set up on Monday, and knew exactly what was going out. Something else I have learned is the idea of layered leadership. One of the biggest things that women deal with is control. We have the hardest time taking our hands-off projects and allowing other people to do them. I think it's because as women, we've always been in the shadow of someone else, but we finally have an opportunity where we can be in the forefront.

We have literally started to implement those practices in our own businesses. The belief that if we have someone work with us and we teach them everything that we know, we're no good anymore and they might steal our secrets has to stop. That's a lie; your power is not really in your accomplishments. Your power is actually in the amount of people you affect. What women have to realize is, the more people we teach who thrive, the more credible we become as entrepreneurs. Don't keep secrets to yourself.

Collaboration is how we grow our networks and credibility as business owners. The more lives I change, the more credible I become. Your credibility will take you places that your gifts and your work ethic can't. If I am working and someone is working with me, I am going to teach that person *every single thing I know*. Who cares if they go out and they become great or successful too? The fact that a person worked with me and I taught them something, and I added value to their life and affected their life so that now they are successful, is just as much a credit to my credibility. That's what people misunderstand. We are so focused on having an effect that we forget it doesn't always have to come from us.

Sometimes our talents can be used to give birth to the next Oprah, or the next Steve Jobs, or the next founder of Walmart. You may mentor that person, and you're just as successful. When you're a speaker, everyone thinks that the person on the stage speaking with the lights shining on them is the most amazing person in the room. But as I've grown, I've been wondering, "Who the hell is the janitor who cleaned this place up, set up the chairs, and set up the audio? That person rocks behind the scenes." Credibility can go in front of the scenes or behind the scenes, and be just as worthy, you know? It's just as equal.

Chapter Two:

Managing Your Time

You could choose to look busy and be broke, or you can manage time well and be productive. Here are my three best tips for time management:

1. Make sure you have your plan in front of you and stick to it. Marketing online is a great thing but the danger is from becoming easily sidetracked. I know when I start scrolling on social media that it's a big distraction. Have you ever gone to a page and hit the "Like" button to find, the next thing you know, you have spent an entire hour scrolling down to pictures from 450 weeks ago? You know? Making sure that I'm not just scrolling is key to my time management, profitability, and success.

2. Set timers and give yourself clear deadlines to complete tasks. This tip keeps me on point and keeps other tasks off my mind.

3. Take regular breaks. Sometimes you have to put your phone down so you can receive and just enjoy life, as well. Taking a break can often lead to increased productivity.

Some people have mastered sitting behind their computer with a fake smile and looking like they're working, but they haven't made a penny all day. Which one are you going to be?

Living in the Microwave World

Nothing happens overnight, especially your business. Anything that does happen overnight won't last. Right now, many people are living in a "microwave" world. Servantship is disappearing because everyone wants to go from rookie to being an expert in a year. You have twenty-two-year-old life coaches who haven't even *had* a life yet. You have "business experts" without any successful businesses. You have people who have rushed the process, and they're not getting their feet wet. They're not going through the journey. They haven't experienced rejection. They haven't had failing companies. They haven't had businesses totally flop so that they had to start over.

Unless you've gone through all that, you're not successful yet. The process isn't easy. We're in a digital age online right now and things are in the beginning. You can kind of manipulate the process; you can even make it look amazing. You can make it look like you're just standing in front of Bentleys and other fancy cars, and you just walk on the beach.

But reality isn't like that. The process includes deciding if you're going to pay rent or buy more products to sell. The process includes losing your apartment and having to stay with a friend because you have something you believe in that no one else sees yet. The process includes taking out payday loans and ducking their calls when you knew from the beginning that you weren't going to pay them back. The process includes starting over without being ashamed that the first effort didn't work and was a total bust. The process includes going to those same friends over and over and over again with a different idea and a different business to the point they run when they see you coming.

These are all the things that people go through that no one talks about. No one talks about the eviction notices. No one talks about your car being repossessed. No one talks about the "Nos," especially the ones that hurt. The "Nos" you get from your friends and the hurt when they buy something similar from someone who's famous instead of from you. The "Nos" from your family members when you ask them to invest in your dream that scar you. All those things are part of the process no one talks about.

They don't talk about watching other people thrive while you are sitting at home posting on Instagram feeling like a complete failure because someone else's business took off faster than yours. They have no experience, and you've been doing it for ten years. This is a part of the process you're going to have to go through, and people are going to have to go through. It's not going to happen in a microwave world. It won't be fixed in a minute. It's going to take a decade or more. You have to be willing to invest that amount of time to truly see those results. That's the process.

Serve Your Way to Success

When you are hungry and thirsty for success, the biggest tip I can offer is to become a student. You are tired of your own excuses and tired of letting fear rule your life, and now you understand that it's going to take more than a minute. Everybody wants to be the teacher, but nobody wants to be the student. Yet the teacher had to be a student before they became a teacher. Right now, we have to go back to servantship. Serve your way to success. Stay around a successful person and figure out what you can bring to their lives, how you can add to what they're doing, how you can learn from them, how you can serve them, and do it for free. Do this rather than trying to find out what you can get from them.

Right now, we are in a place where everyone wants to know how *you* can make *them* successful.

Very few are saying, "How can I get around you to help you become more successful, so I can get that wisdom and experience?" Everyone wants to just skip the experience. It's because the word "boss" is being thrown around like it's the coolest thing you can ever be. The coolest thing you can ever be is the assistant to the most successful person, because you're learning from someone who's wise and knows exactly what they're doing. Understand this about an assistant: they have a front row seat to their boss's life. We have to get back to valuing that vantage point.

Take the Time to Build Relationships

Many people reach out to me online, and the first thing they want to know is if they can pick my brain. When you want to learn from someone, figure out how you can help them. They don't need you. You need to find out how you can add value to what they're doing. When I look for mentors and I need something from someone, I need to figure out how I can help them. What do they need me for? If I have something, I'm not going to try to sell it; I'm going to give it to you. I'm going to help you so much that you're going to see a need for me. That is the mindset they need to have. Go back to the servantship. Serve someone who is in your field, in your niche market. Do it for free without expecting something in return. Being allowed to be in their presence is payment. You are getting wisdom and knowledge. That's the pay.

Recently someone emailed me and offered me one of their t-shirts. I responded graciously and said, "Okay. I just want to make sure that you want to give it to me. Because a lot of people who give me products are expecting free marketing on my page. I just want to be clear that if you want to leverage my platform to make money, that's advertisement, and we need to have a different conversation."

She replied, "No. I just want to give it to you." I sent her my address. She never sent me the t-shirt. People like this are not relationship-building at all. And they don't realize that's why they're not successful. They think that going forward, being a "go-get-it girl" is what's going to make the difference for them.

Remember that old saying, "It's not what you know, it's who you know"? It's an example of when I see people in positions that may not be qualified for on paper. They have built a relationship with someone who knows their heart and knows they have real-world, school-of-hard-knocks qualifications plus loyalty, dedication, and hard work. That boss feels as though they're deserving, either because they've invested time in them or they've done something for them. They feel like that employee is worthy of it. That saying, "It's not what you know, it's who you know" is very important.

Right now, if you are trying to grow your businesses and get people to buy from you, you cannot skip the relationship-building phase. I call this the seed-planting portion. If you don't plant a seed in the ground, and you don't water it, how can it succeed? Watering it is what's going to make it grow, right? If it doesn't get water, the seed isn't going to produce fruit. When you meet someone, if you don't nurture the relationship, how is that relationship ever going to grow? If you go to a social event and get someone's number, but don't call to talk to them or go out for lunch, the relationship will never evolve.

Before you try to shove a sale down a consumer's throat, take the time to get to know them. Take the time to figure out what their goals are, but most importantly, how you can help them through what you plan to offer them. Sometimes we are distracted by our personal goals, which in this case would be the personal goal of landing a sale. Nurturing a relationship and building a relationship will go well beyond that; it will take you (the professional) into the area of client retention while the amateur will focus on just getting the sale. When the amateurs get the sale, they're excited and they celebrate. The pro, the veteran, the person who is more experienced, does not celebrate on the initial sale; they celebrate when the customer comes back again and again and again. That happens because the seller developed a relationship with that customer. They've arrived at a place where that customer trusts them. It's the most important part of the sales process. In our microwave world, many want to skip it, but if you want to be wildly successful, you have to take the time to nurture your relationships. If you take the time to get to know people and build relationships, you will build a bigger customer base and have more support.

I tell people online all the time that you just can't cram a product down someone's throat. I don't care what your business is. The consumer doesn't care. What the consumer cares about is how the product has helped you. What the consumer cares about is what their product has done for you. The consumer cares to see you with it. They want to see the process. I don't simply post photos of what I'm selling online. I *show* people how I'm using it, what it's doing for me, how it makes me look, how it makes me feel, how it's benefited other people. I want testimonials. People want to see the change in how it's impacting other people. That's what marketers are missing.

When I talk to people, I *want* to connect. I may know your name, but I need to know a person's last name. I don't know their kids or how old they are, but I want to know when their children's birthdays are. What dates do they fall on? You need to know their anniversary. You need to know their favorite color. You want to know what makes them go. When people reach out to me for business, I want to know why they want to start a business. What's their motivation behind being an entrepreneur outside of the money? I want to know the emotional tie to the business and the brand they're starting. Those are the questions and the things that we need to ask. Take the time to develop the relationship. Engage. If you're online, comment on those photos. Respond back to them.

If a person sends you an inbox message, talk to them. People who send me messages are shocked when I respond. It's crazy that they're shocked I responded. It just lets me know that people have gotten too damn cool for themselves, as if the less you respond, the cooler you are. Are you in business to be popular or paid? If you're in business to be popular and cool, and you don't want to talk to people and you want to come off appearing better than others, then you're not going to end up being paid. If you're in business to really help people, that's going to take some relationship building. You need to respond to your customers. They are yours now. You may look at them or people messaging you in your inbox like they're bugaboos, but those people are your future customers. They may even be your future friends. They may be people who have answers that you're overlooking. I see this happen a lot.

When I look at the social media pages of some businesses and see one hundred comments but no one from the company has replied or even liked the comment, I can't help but think, "Look at all this business they're missing out on." It will make a person's day if someone from that business just says, "Thank you so much."

When I dedicate time in my business to respond or like each comment on my page, it increases engagement and people respond to that. They realize, "Oh my gosh, her head is not so far up her own bottom that she can't respond to me." She is a real person. It impresses them, and they remember.

Why Consistency Produces Success

Contrary to what a lot of people think; it's not about being the richest person in the room, or even smartest person in the room, or the person who has the tools. Creating success is a big deal but maintaining success is the biggest part of it. In order to maintain success you have to fall in love with doing what you are doing, over and over again. The more consistent a person is, the more successful that person will become, because there is a certain amount of determination and drive instilled in them just to have the ability to get up and do something every single day.

There is a level of passion that has to be tied into people's pursuits for them to be able to get up and do a job over and over again. Right now, many people don't have a lot of discipline. They don't have a lot of consistency. And the person who is the smartest or the person who has the best tools isn't going to be the most successful. It's actually going to be the person who has the power to get up and work it, and make it happen day in and day out. That person is going to see more results than you any day because when you're not passionate about what you're doing, you won't have enough interest. You won't have the excitement of getting up every single day and doing it. It is going to wear off unless the passion is there, unless the consistency is there. That is how I learned to work like I do. I literally have a schedule for every single thing I do, and I get up every single day and do it.

Slow and steady wins the race; that's my outlook on consistency. At one point I was very inconsistent in my business. I would do something, I would get results, but then I'd break my routine. I'd wait until it got bad or my income decreased and then I was scrambling to fix it. Don't wait for everything to fall apart before deciding you need to plan for consistency. Plan for the falling apart and get your ducks in a row.

I learned that I couldn't operate in chaos. I had to get up every day and continue to plant the seeds. When I started to do something every day to plant those seeds in my business, I started seeing the harvest from actions I had taken two years earlier. It was coming full throttle. If I hadn't been doing something every day towards growing and building my business, I would not have been able to see the fruits of my labor.

One time I planted an apple tree in the back yard of my house. I thought when I planted that apple tree that I was going to have apples all over the tree by spring. Then one spring, I looked up to see I had these teeny little balls on the branches of my apple tree. Two years later.

I didn't know it took an apple tree that long to mature. I had been watering it, adding new soil, and nurturing that tree consistently. I was about to give up. I was about to say forget this tree; I'll never have apples. I accept it and I'm over it. But I kept on watering that tree. I kept on making sure fresh soil was around it. I was pruning the tree consistently and ultimately my consistent hard work paid off; there were little apples coming in (and squash too).

You may not get results immediately. But the reward is when you've done it for so long on a consistent basis, you'll get the overflow that comes from what you did years ago.

Chapter Three:

You Get What You Settle For

Your confidence determines their confidence in you. I remember as I was starting in the direct sales industry I often let the opinions of other people influence me. Some even had the gall to suggest, "Oh, you won't be successful in this and no one's going to buy that crap. It's a joke." If you allow other people's perceptions and their thoughts to get in your head, it will slow you down. It took my confidence down a bit in the beginning. The most dangerous thing you can do is believe you *can't* do something or believe you're weak, when you stop being confident in yourself and stop believing in yourself. That tends to happen especially when you listen to other people.

In the beginning, I was very slow to promote and share my business with people because I had already allowed a lack of self-confidence to creep in from listening to others. What I started to notice was the lack of response. When I used to post online, it came off as desperate. "I need you. I need you to buy this. I need you to support this business." I was begging because my confidence wasn't there. At one point, I sat down to look over my bills and realized I needed some help. "Let me see how many people I can get to help me out." I was at a very tough spot in my life then. I called around and only one person was there to help me. My mom. At that time I probably had a bag of turkey wings in my refrigerator and some Oodles of Noodles ramen. When I called everyone, and no one could do anything for me but my mom, it made me realize that I had to stop listening to the opinions of other people and start believing in myself again. That's when the lightbulb went off in my head.

I'm *not* going to be afraid to post my products and promote my business. I'm *not* going to be afraid to say that a certain product is amazing. I'm *not* going to be afraid to claim that I am going to be successful.

I was listening to people who couldn't do a thing for me—why? Because I was worried about what those people were going to say or how those people were going to look at me for attempting to be successful? They were looking down on me for trying to promote something and do something better in my life. Did I want to be connected to these people? When I made that mental shift and started speaking positively, I started affirming success over my life. I started believing that my business and I were going to the top. I started telling people that if they didn't partner with me now they were going to be left out. I started making people feel if they weren't a part of it, if they weren't going after it, if they weren't doing it, if they didn't believe it, then *they* were lacking vision. That's when they started to believe. They started supporting me. They started buying my products. They started saying let me support her business or they started trying. They wanted to support me then, just in case I actually did become successful.

That's normally how it happens. If you don't have confidence in yourself, people can see that. People can see when their own doubt can manipulate you, when it can make you question your goals. If you don't believe in yourself then they're not going to believe in you either. You can sell freaking tissue on a stick if you're confident and believe that tissue on a stick can make a difference. It's your confidence, even when it comes to relationships. If you are not confident in yourself then you'll settle for less. People know when you're not confident and you'll let them to walk all over you. The day you start believing in yourself, in being confident in yourself, and speaking affirmations over yourself and actually believing you deserve success, you are going to see a transition in how people take to you, receive you, respect you, and how they align themselves with you.

When I met my husband, I was at the place in my life where I was not willing to take any more crap from men. My standards were high. I had zero tolerance. If you weren't what I was looking for, you were going to get scratched off the list. When I met the man, who would later become my husband, he knew I had standards because I had put them out there on the table. My husband told me he married me because of those standards. He had dated women in the past but no one called him out on his crap the way I did. The way I stood up for myself and knew exactly what I did and didn't want appealed to him. Knowing I wasn't willing to settle was an attractive, strong feature he respected.

It blew my socks off. I didn't know. I thought, you mean to tell me that I spent my life out here dating and letting things just kind of be swept under the table, and I got what I settled for? When I turned that confidence button on and started believing in myself, I started to get the results I wanted in *every* area of my life. Love, income, and friendship.

Chapter Four:

Live Below Your Means

Sometimes I think about my own success when I look at other business owners. When I was first starting out, I had a "hobby" business, right? Some of the women that I coached were married to engineers who were making six figures a year, so if their businesses weren't making money it was no big deal. Their husbands were still paying the rent. As far as being a single woman, one of the things for which I've been grateful is that there was no one else, just me. I was a single mom with no safety net and no choices. But when I'm in a situation where there's only a bag of chicken thighs in the fridge and Ramen Oodles of Noodles in the cupboard, I know I'm going to go hungry if I don't pick up that phone and make that sales call.

I've been grateful for that because if I'd had a husband who'd said, "Oh don't worry, baby," then I might not have fought so hard for my business.

If I'd had the rent covered by someone else then it wouldn't have pushed me. I'd really like to speak to the women reading to say you've got to create your *own* safety net, have your own savings account, and don't quit your day job until you've got income that's replacing your salary.

Also, don't depend on a man. That's not to say you can't depend on your husband but what happens if one day your husband wakes up and says he doesn't love you anymore. What are you going to do? I've seen so many moms in that situation. They started to live comfortably and had the big house and husband who was making six figures. Then he comes home out of the blue and says he wants a divorce. You don't know where to start. You need to make sure you have some sort of income of your own. Make sure you are creating a savings account you never touch. Think about it.

Pick one: a five thousand-dollar Chanel bag or five thousand dollars in the bank? I think five thousand dollars in the bank for five years will do more for you than that purse. Before you start making those kinds of choices, make sure you have a safety net in place. I meet a lot of entrepreneurs who don't even have a life insurance policy, who don't have health insurance, who don't have wills set up. These are things that you have to put in place, especially if you have kids.

With respect to retirement plans, you don't need to have a job to invest in a 401k; did you know that? There are a lot of people who don't realize you can contribute towards your own retirement plan even as an entrepreneur, and you should; it's a big deal. These are some of the things we have to do to get prepared. Something else I want to say is when you start making a lot of money, live below your means. People often start making more money but they also start creating more bills.

People start going hog wild crazy. Just because you start making more money doesn't mean you have to create more bills. It's like you've got a big house, but you need a bigger house, and then a bigger house, and an even bigger house. Or you get a new car and then another new car. Those things are temporary fulfillment. Every time you turn around you're going to need something else until you realize that you're complete without stuff. You have to be able to see it in your bank account versus living in it and driving around in it.

I waited four years to buy my home, a home that I really wanted. I didn't jump out there and just buy one. I want my assets to be separate from what I'm living in. I want my assets to make me money. If I'm living in it, it's not making me any money—it's overhead. Your mental processes have to shift and this again goes back to confidence. When you're truly confident with who you are, where you are in your life, and what your mission is, stuff does not define you. It just doesn't. You'll make smarter decisions with your money because you're fulfilled.

You Don't Have to Keep Up with People

You are going to go broke trying to prove to people that you're richer than them. Focus on what matters to *you*. Do you have a dream for your life? Start to plot it out, make a plan, implement it, stay focused, and don't get distracted by the bright shiny objects, the flashy cars, the newest gadget, or keeping up with the neighbors.

Start a business. Buy some land. Get something that's going to make you money. Stop buying inconsequential items. I have *three pairs* of shoes. One pair I bought my first year of being successful, as a treat, because I'd never had squat. All of my purses are old; I haven't bought a bag in four years. It's like you have to grow out of that consumer mindset or you'll go broke. People don't realize that. I watch all these people come in from other companies, make all this money, and then it's over. They are driving fancy cars and have big homes, and from outward appearances, they are successful. Then it ends and—yeah—they have no savings. They'd thought the gravy train was going to go on forever and they're right back where they started. I promised myself and my children I'd never be that person.

Promise yourself you won't be that person. Act as if you're still broke. Act as if you are still in your first year of being profitable. Don't go out there trying to keep up with the Joneses. That would be a *big* mistake. Act as if you don't have money. Create an account into which you deposit money but *don't touch it.* You don't even want to know it's there.

Money will show you exactly who you are. And if you don't have any self-discipline, it will make you into a monster. It *will* make you into a monster, where you start to feel as if "stuff" makes you more powerful...when it really doesn't. Your heart, your character, your integrity—how you treat people—mean more than money any day. You can't buy those.

Chapter Five:

Taking the Next Step

I had so many people coming to me with different business opportunities and different things they thought I would be good at. And the truth was, they saw my drive, they saw my dedication level, they saw how committed I was when I put my mind to something. It was that part of me they admired the most. They wanted to use those things for their benefit.

At one point in my life, I was broke. And when you're broke, you will literally consider doing anything to make a dollar. It's the biggest mistake you'll make in your life. I've seen people say, "Yeah, I'm a photographer. Yeah, I'm a writer. I'm your stylist. I can take your pictures. I can do your marketing."

You continue to add on all these services. People do that because they're hungry for a dollar. But you will dominate if you just stay consistent with what you're good at, by staying in your lane. Stay in your lane and you'll never crash. That's what I tell people. And why is that? Because you're most confident and most comfortable when you're doing something you're passionate about, something you enjoy, something that interests you.

But when you are doing things that don't interest you, when you are doing things just for that dollar, the passion is not there. You're not present. It's all about work to make the money, work to make the money, work to make the money. You forget about a lot of the things that are important, such as people. How you make people feel. Your sole focus is literally just money.

I have learned that when I've had people do things that they have no interest in, it's always just about money. They are willing to risk their passions. They are willing to do things they are so uncomfortable with, all for a dollar. When you are operating in your purpose, when you're operating in your gift, you're clear. You can hear from God. You can affect people's lives. You can have clarity.

Have you ever done something you don't like to do? Did you dread it? I remember working in corporate America and dreading every minute while I was driving to that office. I had to be there at 9:00 but I would sit in my car until 8:57, waiting to the last minute to go in. I was dragging myself in just for the dollar. I had no interest.

Every second I could goof off or not work, I would take. I would have my computer screen open on some internet site where I was reading about something I loved. My manager would walk around the corner and I would minimize the screen. I hated being there. But I was there because I was desperate for the dollar; I needed to pay my bills.

Okay, I would also say that when you're not in your lane, you jump. I see people every time I turn around working some different business. They're offering a different service.

They're a different person. Their branding is changing, their message is changing so often. It's truly because they're not staying in their lane. They're all over the place.

When you jump, you quit, you give up. It's like, are you searching to operate in your purpose? Or are you looking to operate in whatever is going to pay you the fastest?

Chapter Six:

The Importance of Transparency

"The two most powerful words when we're in struggle: me too."
—Brené Brown

When I started sharing the things I used to be embarrassed about, people started relating to me and gravitating to me. I took those fears and all the things I was embarrassed about and made a conscious choice to no longer allow judgment of others to control me. Few have ever been brave enough to put their crap out there, and people need that. People are waiting for someone else to say, "Hey. You're not alone. I'm drowning over here in my finances too. My love life is same $&@#, just like yours. Your business is failing? Oh, mine is too." People need that. When you're transparent, they are attracted to you like a magnet. In addition to drawing others to you, you can establish relatability, credibility, and trust. As women, we are taught to put on the "fake joker face."

We know how to pretend as if everything is fine. We appear happy. We can pack a load of makeup on our faces to make us look good.

We don't realize that it's okay to go through hell. We don't realize that we are all dealing with something. Now I'm being booked and paid to speak on stages and tell the same, embarrassing story that I was once ashamed of. *People are actually paying me to come and share it on their stage.* It's mind-blowing. Why? Because I didn't realize the power of transparency by showing and telling people all the crap I went through. Even from a spiritual standpoint of freedom, people can be free from all the things they're dealing with once they realize that someone else has dealt with it as well. You know?

I started sharing parts of my story piece by piece. First, I wanted to share that I was a teen mom. Then I started sharing that I grew up in a crack house. Then I started sharing about my love life fiascos, how I was in a relationship and invested a lot of time in it and when it didn't work out, the disappointment I felt. I started to share *me* piece by piece. I noticed the more I shared, the more I attracted women who had experienced those same things. Share more and you can attract more people who are going through the same thing or have gone through the things that you're talking about. Does that make sense?

I initially started sharing one-on-one, letting my friends and staff know, "You're not alone. I've been there too." It quickly grew to sharing with groups. People started asking me to share that story at their events. I would hear things like, "Women here have this feeling like it's the end of the world, and they need to realize it's not the end of the world."

If you're sharing online, one of things that I recommend you make sure you do is to be transparent. It's so important that you are transparent and put yourself out there. Sharing online is going to free somebody else who's embarrassed. Transparency is going to allow people to see you are human, just like them, and they'll respect you. They will see you're not that type of person who has to pretend like life is perfect.

People want to see your imperfections, so don't be afraid to show your imperfections. Don't be afraid to show that you fall short. Don't be afraid to share online some of those mistakes and things that you've made in life because it is going to free someone else. You are the vessel for the information and freedom. You know what I'm saying? Who cares about how screwed-up what you were doing was? People just want to hear that it happened, even to you, and what you learned from it. It's ok to share with others the poor choices that you've made, the uncomfortable moments you've experienced, how you've screwed up and the lessons that you have learned as a result of it.

Chapter Seven:

That Leap of Faith in Yourself

So many people come to me about starting a business and the first thing they talk about is taking out a gigantic loan. "I want to start a business. I need to take out twenty-five thousand to thirty thousand dollars to get my business off the ground." I look at people and ask them what they are thinking! That's a lot of debt to put yourself in for a first-time business that may not even thrive. *You* have to take that risk.

I invested a few hundred dollars to start my business; there will always be risks that come with starting any business. The key is knowing that in business you having to reinvent yourself over and over, but the risk will remain.

You'll risk putting out different products and waiting to see if people like them or they don't. Heck, business comes with a lot of different things that people tend to overlook. You're going to have to take the risks when it comes to your family and your friendships. This is working the process. Definitely work the process.

I took a risk and quit my job, even with three kids. I quit a government job with security and health insurance and everyone thought I was nuts, including my mom.

I took a risk when starting one boutique with five hundred dollars to my name. I didn't know if it was going to turn around, if I was going to make a profit. But I did it. All the things I took a risk on turned out to be the most successful things, every time.

When *you* take a risk and it doesn't work out, that's not failure. You simply earned something!

When you take those risks and things don't work, it doesn't mean that it's over. I want readers to know that it means they should go back to the beginning, start over, and come back again.

And we're back to staying in your lane.

Chapter Eight:

Trials Create Your Resume

I used to be embarrassed when I would try but still fail at something. You know, I got slammed. I used to think that was embarrassing. Then I started to realize the more I went through, the stronger I became. The more businesses that failed, the more marketing that sucked, the better I revamped my campaigns to come back as a stronger marketing campaign. The more relationships that failed in my life, the more my standards increased and the more I expected from the men I dated. My story and the experiences I went through gave me credibility.

These experiences about failure taught me never to confuse what I was offered with what I was worth. Many times in my life, I was a low-shooter. That is, I was afraid to ask for more. I failed to realize I *could* have more. I always underbid in areas of my life. Even in business, I would always set my prices way too low. My expectations about men were very low at one time in my life. The same with regard to marketing and putting myself out there. How you do anything is how you do everything.

I had so much experience in so many different departments that it was almost impossible for me to talk to someone and not have something valuable to offer.

"Hey. I know how I can empower you." Your experience encompasses your entire life. Not just work experiences, but friendship experiences, mother experiences, wife experience. My experiences made me stronger. It builds your credibility and builds that resume up for you. It shows other people that you're strong, that you're smart, that you're gifted with something, and that you're an overcomer. And that's a big deal.

See Failures as Learning Opportunities

I created my makeup line in my home, I went out and sold it to people, and they bought it. What happened over time was I didn't have the finances that I needed to manufacture the product, develop good packaging, ship it internationally, or do everything else that a flourishing business has to deal with. After a while, it got to a point where I was filling all those jars up and packaging all that *by myself.* I couldn't take anything else on. My fingers were burning. I came to the conclusion that I needed to find a company that would store my products in-house and ship it out for me versus me doing the boxing, mailing, and shipping.

That is kind of how that worked for me or didn't work for me. Watching that business fail, watching that business flop and realizing I thought I could do it and getting towards the end and realizing I didn't have the capital to succeed, realizing I didn't have the manufacturer to do it. It was a lightbulb moment. *Failures.* We all have to go through them to get to the other side.

I failed at being an office manager while attempting to lead people who were sometimes twenty years older than I was. They chewed me apart; that was the first thing. I failed at it because I wasn't good at it—I wasn't good at being a team player. It was the blame game for me and it got me to a place where it made people question my leadership skills at work. I had to really touch them up and apply those to business as well.

I also failed at trying to write a book without sharing my true testimony and my true story behind it. It failed because I wasn't being true to who I was, and wasn't showing my real self, you know? I had to start all over again.

Initially I wanted to keep the book more general and tried to avoid sharing my whole story. I've been wanting to share my story for a very long time, but I was concerned about being judged for things, such as being a young mother or growing up in a drug house. I didn't know if people would listen to me if I put that in a book.

The outcome of this process was understanding that I was being used as a vessel versus being this perfect person, and understanding that perfection doesn't exist. In order for you to share your story and to get the response you want from an audience, you're going to have to share your truth and that includes your failures. You can't sugarcoat your truth to be whatever you want it to be that day, you have to tell the real stuff. Because truth is going to draw people to you who may have gone through the exact things that you've gone through.

Chapter Nine:

How to Deal with Hate

Can I be honest for a minute? You will be talked about and hated on. For those who smile in your face, just know that not everyone will genuinely like you. When you start accomplishing the dreams and goals you have, and your successes are being noticed worldwide it can be tough knowing who is really for you. It's sad but it will happen!

You can't avoid back stabbers when dealing with success and people. Sometimes you'll just want to crawl under a rock and hide for a while.

But I have a few things to share that will help you with these situations.

1. Stay mindful of your emotions

Dealing with someone who rubs you the wrong way can have a negative effect on your own emotions. A toxic person can drive you crazy, but only if you let them. Remember, only you have power over your emotional state. Don't allow a negative or toxic person to influence your state of mind. That doesn't mean that you ignore the person or disregard how they make you feel. Recognize when your emotions, such as irritation and annoyance, are scaling up. If someone is making you angry, let yourself feel that emotion and then let those feelings dissipate. And remember, sometimes all you need to do is smile and nod. There's no need to engage.

2. Choose tact over temper

Learn to cultivate a diplomatic poker face—this is key to learning to treat all people with civility and politeness. It doesn't mean you have to agree with someone you dislike or go along with what they say. You just need to maintain a consistent level of decorum when interacting with them.

3. Don't take it personally

Often people do what they do because of themselves, not because of you. They may be reacting to something in their own circumstances, and it's just a coincidence that you ended up in their crosshairs.

4. Rise above the irrational

It's easy to react emotionally to a toxic person, especially if their behavior seems ridiculous and frustrating. But if you stoop to their level and become embroiled in disputes, you may also be labeled a troublemaker. Don't let your emotions get the best of you or allow yourself to be consumed by their antics. Remember, you don't need to respond to their chaos. You can choose to rise above it by focusing on facts and rational responses. Point out specific issues or problems if need be, but do so diplomatically.

5. Calmly express your feelings

Often, it's the way we communicate that leads to bigger problems. If someone's behavior and communication style annoy you, it may be time to have an honest talk about how you feel. The key is to do so calmly and in a non-confrontational but assertive way.

Non-accusatory language involves making "I" statements. The goal is to clearly and non-aggressively express how you feel and their role in your current state without blaming them. One formula you can use goes like this. "When you _____, I feel _____. Please do this instead: _______."

Be as specific as possible when telling someone which behaviors make you upset and what you would like them to do to correct the problem. Once you've expressed yourself, be open to hearing their side.

6. Pick your battles.

Not all things are worth your time and attention. Sometimes dealing with a noxious person is like reasoning with a toddler in a tantrum: They just don't deserve your energy or engagement. Ask yourself if you really want to get caught in a protracted argument about an issue you can sidestep. Is the ultimate benefit worth the challenge? Do you have more to lose than win?

Consider if the issue is situational, in which case it may dissolve or dissipate with time. Sometimes a quarrelsome person serves to benefit us in other ways. It may be in your best interest to put up with their idiosyncrasies if they are helping you more than hurting you.

Most common mistakes: Leaping too soon

What are some other common mistakes you might face? One is quitting your job too quickly. Another is impatience or overspending before you're sure that something is in your budget. Not running the proper analytics, not being financially stable, or changing directions too soon.

As you grow and prosper, you're going to see a lot of people compare their lives to you and it's going to be like, "Oh, she's driving her dream car and I'm not right now." They'll look at you and develop a certain opinion of you. Some will feel like, "Why not me? Why can't I do that?"

You'll deal with outgrowing people. That happens a lot. You may have people in your life with whom you're super close prior to starting a business and becoming successful, but as time progresses you realize, "Man, I don't even have that person's phone number stored in my phone anymore. I'm not talking to that person as much as I used to talk to them," because you're busy.

You'll get busy and you'll need to be around other people who can relate to you. People who are just as busy, people who are entrepreneurs. I've gone through a lot of that. After I had a lot of growth people were like, "You've changed." I'm like, "Oh yeah, I'm sorry. I was done being miserable with you, babe." That's the biggest thing. Many will want to keep you where you are. They feel more comfortable with you being beneath them.

Success Story

My biggest success story is my best friend, Lela. When I met her, she was so timid and didn't believe in herself. She had worked at her job for over ten years and always thought of her talents as "just small" gifts, and didn't realize that she had the power to leverage those gifts. Through working with her and her passion for dance, I gave her a gentle nudge off the cliff and said, "Hey, you're starting a dance company." I helped her to get her business going. Here are the steps we followed:

1. I evaluated her business and encouraged her to put something out there. (That is often the scariest part for every entrepreneur.)
2. We put together sell packages for her business that I would be interested in personally as a consumer.
3. We made sure it was affordable but also worth it for her. This is something that not a lot of entrepreneurs take a time to look at. Make sure that the time you have to put into a new business is worth it for you.
4. We asked other people to share. Don't be afraid to ask people to post and share news of your business on their marketing and social media. The worst they can say is "No."
5. We asked on our social media platforms who would be interested in "something like this" (the offer we'd created) and then circled back with those people and brought them on as clients.
6. We started rolling out the marketing. I will teach you how. It is outlined at the end of this book.

And Lela's business has continued to thrive. She has over two hundred kids in her dance program now.

August 1, 2017, was her last day at work. She was afraid to quit her job for such a long time, and to see her finally step out and do it and not be fearful touched my heart. I am so happy for her. That happiness from quitting her job and being around a person who is now so passionate about what they do is a deep privilege. She's so great with children and really loves teaching dance. She loves the excitement her students experience when they're dancing with her and she's involved.

Her company is now grossing six figures. She is one of the first people I offered to help. It took two or three years, though. It doesn't happen in a minute and you don't have to quit your job right away. If you would like the opportunity for personal coaching with me, please go to my website and complete an application form.

Chapter Ten:

The Most Common Mistakes

The most important advice I would offer you if you are wanting to branch out and start your own business is to wait and be patient. Lela was a success because I taught her not to be so anxious to quit her job. I believe that many people often feel like they're invincible and can take on the world. They find themselves saying, "I can do this and I'm ready to fight and I'm firing my boss," and all this stuff that everyone is putting out there online. In reality, you're being financially irresponsible, and that's a fact. If you go out and quit your job and think that business and customers are just going to fall in your lap, you're going to have another thing coming.

What happens when your electricity gets disconnected? What happens when your car gets repossessed? What happens when you get an eviction notice? All because you rushed the process of growing a solid business and quit your job. You're not going to be able to pay your cellphone bill, and then you're going to end up having to find someone who will let you live with them until you get back on your feet. Be patient.

In her own words

I wanted you to hear from Lela herself what the experience was like for her. Since 2011, Lela Wilhite has been living her dream running a dance studio program for children ranging in age from eighteen months to thirteen years old. She teaches ballet, tap, and hip hop. She also has an adult program to teach women how to be confident, fit, and sexy while learning choreography in high heels.

Prior to running this business, she was a full-time human resource manager. She resigned in August 2017 to pursue her dance program full-time. She was asked to stay and is now contracted out as one of their HR consultants. This is what happens when your purpose aligns with your actions: you become a magnet, and everyone wants to work with you.

Lela has always been in the creative arts. She has always been goal driven and wanted to get back into dance, but she didn't know how to put a plan together or how to execute it. She also says she didn't have the push. "I always wanted to teach dance but I didn't think I would ever be successful at it because I thought I had left it too late. I thought I should have started in my twenties or early thirties."

But it's never too late.

"Now that I'm older," Lela says, "I believe everything happens for a reason. Now that I have all my tools in place, my qualifications, my skill set, my operational component, I see that I am at where I'm at because of my age, because I had the maturity to follow through with what I started."

The biggest challenge that Lela faced before she implemented the tools I share in this book was having the confidence to know she can accomplish whatever she puts her mind to. "Ronne, your expertise and tools elevated my business to the next level. I had to learn so much while I transitioned, but confidence is key. In the beginning, I struggled the most with marketing and branding myself. And the expertise you share in this book helped my business grow from five students to now more than two hundred in my program.

"I think you are a living example of success. You always model the advice you give. You have not told me anything that you do not do yourself. I can look at your social media and implement the strategies you are using in your own business. I don't take your ideas but knowing how you grew your platform has helped me to mimic your social media strategies and branding while speaking to different audiences."

Lela says that her biggest realization on this journey is that once you actually kick fear to the curb you can conquer anything. "Use every obstacle as a stepping tool to get to where you want. Many life events happened throughout my transition in growing my business. However, I could not let them deter me or stop me or slow me down. I just kept going."

Lela learned to use any of the negativity to lift her up. "Whatever life is giving you or whatever circumstances you're in, allow that to be a platform to elevate and grow into your business. And then get rid of that stinking thinking. You always have to have a positive mindset. Your mind literally determines how far you will go in life."

Share an example of a time where you were facing a challenging circumstance you weren't sure you would overcome.

I had a specific goal around reaching a certain number of students in my dance program. My numbers weren't where I wanted them to be, and I was panicking and frantic. I had overhead, I had expenses. There were items I needed to purchase in order to keep running the business, but my revenue just wasn't generating properly. You said we had to work on changing my mindset and my entire thought process.

One of the first things you always tell me is, "Get out of the mindset of making money. It's good to want dollars; it's good to want the revenue to generate, but if you get out of the mindset of thinking about dollars and switch your thinking towards what you can do for somebody else (or how you can help them, a service you can provide), that is how your revenue will automatically increase. Focus on other people."

I started focusing on how to utilize my passion to help a child who wants to dance, who wants to learn hip hop, who wants to elevate their dance career to the next level, or to help a young adult feel sexy and confident. Shifting focus from my numbers meant learning how to dive into my passion, help the community, and make the kids number one, give them an outlet to be creative, want to dance, to learn how to have fun. Once I started focusing on my purpose, things totally took off.

Don't Quit Your Day Job

I was building the business for six years before I left my HR job. I waited until I got to a certain income level with my business before I left. There is life, still. You still have to be able to cope and deal with everyday life, with things that may come at you. Your car may break down, your kid may need extra funds so make sure your priorities are straight first.

Everything is not going to be perfect, everything is not going to occur at the right time. But you'll know when it's time to elevate to the next level. I had Ronne's sustained support over that six years. Even if you don't have access to Ronne directly, find a mentor or a business advisor or someone to guide you along the way to make sure that you know when that time is right.

Educate Yourself

Stay up-to-date on the trends and current information in your niche or industry. Read what other successful entrepreneurs are doing in your field. How can you be more innovative? How can you be creative? I do a lot of research in the dance arena to make sure I'm staying updated to where I can remain afloat in my business.

If you're confident in the product or service you are providing, you have to really own it. Of course, you have to do the legwork; you can't be lazy. And one of the keywords that Ronne is saying all the time is be consistent. You can't pop up here and there and think your business is going to grow overnight. Start with baby steps, be consistent, and you are going to make it.

—Lela Wilhite, Owner/Artistic Director,
Lela Belles Studio of Dance

Here are some other mistakes I see:

1. Underselling. Not charging what you are worth.
2. Not taking the time to build relationships and offer value first.
3. Failing to conduct market research. Putting out a product that *you* like rather than something that others like and are willing to buy.

For example, prior to creating the Girl CEO Planner, a planner to help more women become organized in their day to day lives, I conducted a test and gave away a free planner for a day. It was a sample printable just to see how many people would respond to the offer and download it. Within one day, a few hundred people had downloaded it. I realized, "Wow, people are really into being organized." I started getting positive feedback about how much they were loving the printable. They began requesting that I create a full year planner. It was so clear that women wanted the planner because they were requesting what I was already thinking about launching. I did my market research first. A big mistake I see is people failing to do the market research first. They keep everything quiet and then roll something out they think is going to be cool, and then no one buys it.

> Get your own copy of the Girl CEO Planner by visiting my website at girlceoinc.com

Nichole Butler is a full-time real estate agent and a successful network marketer. She has been in the real estate business since 2013 and in network marketing since 2015. Before that, she was a correctional officer working in a prison for seven years. She used Girl CEO Planner to completely transform her life.

Can you describe what life was like for you before you left your day job and started being an entrepreneur full-time?

Working as a correctional officer was incredibly stressful, and I would bring that stress with me when I got home to my children. I would need thirty minutes to an hour to myself just to switch from work mode to home mode. When I walked through my front door, I had to turn into a whole different person; I couldn't be a correctional officer with my kids. It also meant I did not spend a lot of time with my children because my job was so demanding. Because I worked so much, we missed vacations and holidays and although it could have been worse, dealing with that atmosphere every day was stressful.

Financially, I was living paycheck to paycheck. Once I paid the bills and fed the kids and covered basic essentials here and there, that was it. I had nothing else. I had to wait another two weeks to get paid again and to do it all over. I wasn't able to save money and I wasn't able to accomplish much working a nine-to-five job even though I was getting paid decent money. Once I left that job and was a year into selling real estate, I was able to accomplish more. I bought my first home. And I bought the home I wanted. I didn't have to crawl before I walked. I was able to take trips. I was able to be more involved with my kids and school just by being home more. My life changed tremendously.

My health improved. When I was working, I was always eating on the go. I was too tired to work out, plan meals, or cook at home. Now I am able to set my own schedule. I am getting up with enough time to cook breakfast without rushing. I can go to the gym anytime of the day. I am able to go to the grocery store, buy and cook food, and have it prepared before the kids come home. Being my own boss has made my work/life balance a lot healthier.

What is the biggest strategy or tip that you learned from me that has made the biggest difference for you?

Ronne, you got me comfortable talking to people. I learned how come out of my shell. I wasn't the type to initiate a conversation, but being around you and seeing you talk to people would rub off on me. *Okay, I can do that.* Now I talk to people like I have known them for years.

You showed me how to market my business on Instagram. With you teaching me the marketing skills for the network marketing business, I realized I could use the same principles and apply them to real estate.

What is it like for you now?

A piece of cake. Right now, everything is running so smoothly. I learned from you how to set daily goals. I purchased your Girl CEO Planner, which helped me put my goals and tasks on paper and get my day in order. The main thing is to actually follow what you write down in the planner. The notes you write today are the blueprints for your wildest dreams.

My biggest realization on this journey is: If you put your mind to something and put it in place, no matter how hard it may seem, no matter how many failures you have, if you just keep going at it, you will be successful.

What would you say to the readers who are struggling and want to be successful but have something standing in their way or are scared to take the first step?

1. **Step out on faith.** At first, I didn't share with a lot of people because I didn't want the naysayers to get in my way. I kept things to myself and just went for it. When I left my corrections officer job, I did not have my real estate license yet. At the time, I was working the night shift from 9:00 p.m. to 5:00 a.m. I took that schedule because I wanted to sell real estate during the day. One day I went to work and found out my shifts were getting switched. The new shift meant I would be working during the day. I didn't complain. I went home and slept on it. I realized this job had helped me long enough. I knew that if I switched shifts, I wasn't going to have the time to do what I really wanted. I spoke with my now-husband and he supported me. I went back to work and gave them my resignation. I just stepped out on faith. Was it tough at the beginning? Absolutely. I didn't get a real estate deal until six months after I got my license. But I refused to give up because I didn't want to put myself back into the situation I had come from.

2. **Expect failure.** Expect things not to work out on the first try. I promise if you continue to move forward, if you keep taking steps, and keep wanting it, it will happen. Be prepared for the negative energy that's going to come from failing. If you want it bad enough, you've got to keep on going. Get those things out of your life that are getting in the way; if they mean you no good, get rid of them. And keep going. No matter how many times you fall, keep getting up. The worst thing that can happen is that you're going to be in a situation that you are in today. You're not going to go any lower. The only thing you can do from this point is go higher.

If your heart is set on something, don't let anything come in the way to change it. Keep fighting for it and stay strong. It will surface.

—Nichole Butler, Full-time entrepreneur

Here are some solutions for those common mistakes:

1. Wait it out. Play chess, not checkers. When you play checkers, you're constantly jumping, making unthinking moves to get to the end as fast as you can. When you play chess, you're thinking about your moves before you make them. All your moves are well planned out. You're focusing on the end goal and that's what you need to do in business. You have to slow down and map out what you're

doing. Work your job while you do your hustle and your passion part-time. Work your hustle until it pays you like your full-time job. Even when it starts paying you like your full-time job, take some time to study the analytics; you might just have gotten lucky and had a good year, and the next year it's slammed.

2. Have a healthy savings account in place. I have seen so many people move into big homes they couldn't afford before they were ready and then five or six years later, their homes have been foreclosed. Sales will be up and down, but your mortgage will be due every month. I have seen so many people refinance and then the value of their home goes underwater. They get to a place where they *have* to file bankruptcy because they moved into a home they couldn't afford. Be safe. Make sure you have enough money in your savings account to cover your mortgage for a year.
3. Take at least a year to work your business while studying the financial trends. You could have one good summer and then the next summer no one buys from you at all, but you've quit your job because you had one good season. Study the trends in your business and see how consistent your customers are. Running a business is not about a one-time sale; it's about creating retention with customers who come back and buy from you and who also refer other people to your business.

Chapter Eleven:

Better to Be Safe, Not Sorry

Before I bought my second home, I was so afraid that my company was not stable enough that I waited to purchase it. I didn't rush; I wanted to see the stability in my business first. I saved so much money by living in my old house that had a mortgage of under fifteen hundred dollars a month. I was making literally my yearly salary a month, close to over half a million a year. People were looking at me wondering, "Why is she still living in that little house? Why didn't she buy a mansion yet?" It was because I did not know the future of my business and I needed to study the trends of my business before I jumped out there and got myself into deeper debt.

I was saving up money. I was preparing. If I bought a home I wanted to be able to cover my home mortgage and costs at any time. I waited four years before I bought a new home...four years of making over five hundred thousand dollars every year versus if I had jumped out there and bought a home beyond my means. Had something gone wrong with my business, I would have been up the creek. But I wanted to see what year one looked like and then what year two looked like, and then year three just to be on the safe side. By the time year four came around I had enough money that even if my business had flopped I could still cover the mortgage on my home.

Making responsible decisions such as not getting too anxious and jumping out there and quitting your job will save your life. It *will* save your life. It is better to be safe than sorry.

Chapter Twelve:

Don't Think Business Is Just About Getting Loans

You can go fast alone, but you will not go far.

Everyone thinks you have to have a business loan but spending money you don't have is a terrible way to run a business. Don't bite off more than you can chew, loans are cheese in a mousetrap. It's so tempting, but going for a loan could harm you. Getting a loan is like watching a mouse go over and take a bike bite of the cheese in the trap; it's a risk, but the mouse doesn't realize it's going to be trapped. Getting that loan sounds amazing but what many don't understand is that you're getting yourself into double the debt. Many people see amount of the loan but not the interest. You don't realize that when you get a loan, you're paying that loan almost twice depending on what that interest rate is. It's the same with cars, and it's the same even financing cellphones. Take a long look at interest rates and understand the actual dollar amount you will be paying. That's why I took the time to wait it out when I bought my home, because I know when you buy a house, you almost buy it twice once you've paid interest. Just paying an extra mortgage payment a year, or an extra one thousand dollars annually on top of your mortgage could really knock down a lot of interest and in addition to that, in can help pay off your home or car faster and save you more money. Think before you make that leap.

"You don't have a business if you're a one-man show, you are a service provider. It takes a team to build a solid business."—Ronne B.

You can go fast alone, but you will not go far. Some people are reluctant to put a team in place and call themselves a business. But, you don't have a business if you're a one-man show. You're a service provider in that case. That's it. You only have a company when you have people using the paddles to make the boat row. It takes a team to build a solid business. A lot of people think they can take the order at the drive-through window, scoop the French fries, put them in the to-go bag, and handle the marketing, all at the same time. You can't. (And they're also going to the farm to grow the potatoes!)

You can't plant the seeds, turn the soil, provide the water, and cultivate the product alone; a team will have your back and b as invested in the business as you are. All for one, and one for all.

If you have learned anything from the previous pages, it is that I believe a person needs to show their truth, their transparency, and their failures before their business can succeed. Once you realize these steps are important to success, you will have a business that flourishes and one you can be proud of to shout about from the rooftops or plaster across social media—Instagram, in fact.

Which leads me to the next section of my book. Pay close attention to the exact steps I followed to make millions online.

Part Two

Chapter Thirteen:

Why Instagram?

What if I told you that each time you post a picture to Instagram that post has the ability to grow your influence, boost your sales, and increase your income?

What if you could post to Instagram and have your business viewed by thousands within seconds? Since launching my Instagram page in 2012, I have been able to build a community 100,000 strong, and I've become recognized as a social media influencer able to turn my business into a multi-million-dollar empire!

And guess what? You can too!

Never in my wildest dreams did I imagine that this former janitor and teen mom could build a seven-figure business in just a few short years, leveraging a *free* social media platform.

I'm just a mom who wanted to find a way to make more money without hustling day and night to find clients and customers; who ultimately discovered the secret to working *smarter*, not harder.

After years of trial and error, I've created a unique and fun way to use Instagram to grow my million-dollar business, and after receiving so many requests, I'm excited to finally be able to share them with you!

Instagram has allowed me to:

- Share my story and journey of going from "mopping floors to making millions."
- Building a social media following of over 100,000 people in under four years.
- Build an email list of over 50,000 people that love my business tools and products and reach out to work with me at every opportunity.
- Automate my marketing and promotion to expand my reach and automate my sales.
- Attract influencers and industry players for collaborations.
- Build a team of over 30k business partners; many of whom have gone on to build their own six- and seven-figure incomes.

Instagram is my go-to social media platform for many reasons. It allows your potential customers to take a peek into your world to see if what you have is something they're interested in. It allows them to engage with you, reach out to you, and get a response. It allows you to market your business, personal brand, and product offerings to people globally. It has effectively allowed me to attract people from all over the world to my business.

Now here's the best part—Instagram can do this for you too!

Every strategy, tactic, and method I use to achieve such amazing results through social media and Instagram, I'm sharing with you in my Instagram Diary.

The way I mapped out this formula is simple:

Step #1: **D** Develop Your Undeniable Digital Brand
Step #2: **I** Image Is Everything: How to Build a Visual Brand That Goes Viral
Step #3: **A** Audience Connection: How to Engage Your Audience with Conversations That Convert
Step #4: **R** Share Real-Life Stories That Showcase Your Products
Step #5: **Y** Yield Massive Profits with Community-Building Collaborations

Now that I have piqued your interest—*Yes!*, you can absolutely attract your ideal customer, grow your business, and build a global community from Instagram.

That is, if you know what to do and how to do it (wink)!

Most people underestimate the power of Instagram but after taking action on the business-building steps I share inside this guide, you will have the know-how to completely slay on Instagram.

Are you ready? Let's get started!

Chapter Fourteen:

Instagram Diary

I know you've seen the mad dash that's taking place on Instagram. Moms are becoming IG rock stars, millennials are becoming millionaires, and it's the one social media site where you can take an idea, post an image, and become an influencer overnight.

Instagram has over 600 million users and is one of the fastest-growing social media platforms on the planet. But for many of you, it's also one of the trickiest to navigate.

For each follower you get, you seem to lose two more, your engagement numbers are shameful, and you have no clue how to turn your images into tangible income. Instagram may not have been good to you up until this point.

Every time you share a picture, you come back, only to find a post with no comments, very few likes, and a whole lot of time wasted. You may be wondering, "Is it me? What am I doing wrong?"

So by now, you're likely to be:

- Frustrated with Instagram and its stupid algorithm for sucking up your time and effort (and having nothing to show for it).
- Annoyed that so many entrepreneurs are "killing it" on Instagram, but you're stuck with useless IG guides, courses, and methods from gurus whom you can't seem to duplicate.
- Sick and tired of hearing about how much money there is to be made on Instagram, because you can't seem to get into the club!
- Ready to give up because you just can't take the disappointment any longer.

How do I know? Because I was *you* just a few years ago.

You see, I saw the value in Instagram from the very beginning when I was trying to build my business as a salon owner, but the game changed when I started growing my home-based health and wellness business.

I wanted a way to help my team grow their businesses, build their influence, and see rapid results without spending a ton of time or money to do it. So I tried, I tested, and I taught myself everything I could about how to leverage Instagram until I landed a system that not only worked for me, but, my business partners too. Systems are a success only when they can produce similar results for other people.

Here is how this **Instagram Diary** works:

Inside this book are five results-driven strategies along with actionable exercises—your IG Diary Entries—that will walk you through the process of turning Instagram into your personal ATM.

Within each chapter, you'll find personal stories and easy-to-implement advice that give you the ins-and-outs of my make-Instagram-profitable-plan.

I suggest you take this **Diary**, block off thirty to forty-five minutes per chapter, and immediately apply what you learn as you create your own customer-grabbing, profit-pulling Instagram account.

Use this **Diary** to write compelling captions. Apply the tips to snap scroll-stopping images.

Use what I teach to turn your Instagram feed into a lead-generation machine.

The bottom line is that once you understand the core concepts and principles behind a profitable Instagram profile, you'll have the power to use Instagram to sell just about anything!

One word of advice before we get started: You invested in this book for a reason, so put it to good use. It took me five years to build my social media account to 100,000, but it doesn't have to take you that long if you implement what I teach. Take immediate and swift action and you can gain momentum in as little as thirty days.

To see results quickly, you have to learn and implement as you go! That means taking action, creating your own Instagram posts as you read each chapter, and doing your own IG **Diary** entries, so you can finally get the results so many other influencers rave about.

Just imagine the type of success you can create and the type of empire you can build! It all starts here and it starts now!

Diary Entry #1

WHAT'S YOUR BUSINESS?

____

____

HOW DO YOU THINK INSTAGRAM CAN HELP YOUR BUSINESS?

____

____

WHAT ARE YOUR INSTAGRAM GOALS?

____

____

WHAT'S YOUR CURRENT FOLLOWER COUNT?

____

____

HOW MANY FOLLOWERS DO YOU WANT IN THREE MONTHS, SIX MONTHS, AND 1 YEAR FROM NOW?

____

____

WHAT TOOLS OR RESOURCES DO YOU NEED TO HELP YOU REACH YOUR GOALS?

____

____

Chapter Fifteen:

Building Your Brand

Instagram is *the* one place where you can *really* show off your personality! Each day you get to share posts that speak to your purpose and passion. I am blown away by the creativity that I see on Instagram. There are entrepreneurs from all walks of life, with different backgrounds, styles, and perspectives on life, who are all making an impact in their own unique ways.

Instagram overwhelms a lot of home-based entrepreneurs because they don't know where to start. They may not be the best photographer. They may feel like they aren't creative or clever enough to "stand out" or come up with compelling captions. They may not have any physical products to show off, or cute Jimmy Choo heels to take an awesome "shoefie."

But that's *okay*! Because building a brand on Instagram isn't just about the perfect lifestyle pic or caption, it's also about the experience you give to your audience, the authenticity and the value given in each post.

Your Instagram account should be an extension of your brand. It should reflect who you are as a wife, a mom, a daughter, a father, a son, a partner, a spouse, and as an entrepreneur.

Every component matters when it comes to how you portray your personal brand on social media. Instagram is no exception. Whether you're sharing a picture of your morning chai latte, your product, or your family vacation, when your photos pop up in someone's feed they should know immediately that they're *your* photos. That's what successful branding is all about!

Your Instagram feed should complement your brand like a large bag filled with enough goodies to make people want to know more about you, your products, and services.

So now that you know why building your brand is important, let's start creating yours!

Step One: Create your Instagram account

Now, more than ever, people are becoming their brand. You must realize that *you* are a walking billboard. When it comes to creating your Instagram account, you have two options:

#1: Use Instagram as a personal account.
#2: Upgrade a personal account to a business account.

Every business is different, so it depends on you. It's up to you to decide how you want to operate and position yourself. If *you are* your business, aka a personal brand, simply turn your personal account into a business account and share a healthy mix of personal and business-related content using the one account. Using Instagram as a business account is important because it now allows you to track your stats.

If you have a business page, you can see how many people are following your page every week, what content people are engaging with, what they like, and it allows you to be more intentional in posting and connecting with your audience.

Step Two: Identify your niche market

What do you want to be known for?

Have you ever landed on someone's Instagram feed, and after scrolling through their page or maybe even after visiting their website, you're still not clear on exactly what it is that they do or how they can even help you?

When it comes to building your personal brand you need to know the Who, Why, What, and How.

WHO do you want to serve?
WHY do you want to serve them?
WHAT benefit will they receive from working with you?
HOW do you deliver that benefit to them?

When you don't clearly define your niche and what you want to be known for, you run the risk of marketing a business that isn't clear about what it really represents.

You can't truly build your authority or expertise without a clear focus, because your followers won't know what you're an expert in! And you can't say that you're an expert at any one thing if you're offering too much to too many people.

Your Instagram community will follow you and ultimately buy into *you*, because they trust that you can be the solution to a very specific problem they have. If they doubt for a second that you can't deliver what they need and want, they will move on to the next person (your competition)! Influencers who make a lot of money on Instagram are able to attract and grow a following because they have been able to establish themselves as the go-to resource in a specific area.

If you want to really grow a targeted and profitable Instagram following, you should narrow your niche, not widen it. For example, when you see my profile, it reflects the following:

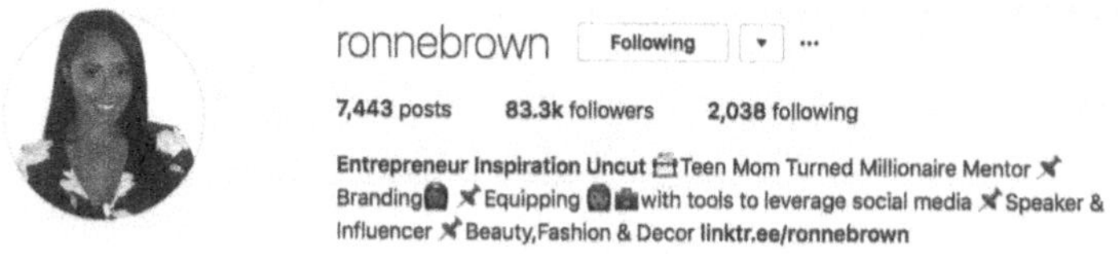

Although you'll want to establish a niche, keep in mind that it's okay to mix personal and business, but be strategic with your personal shots knowing that every post you make leaves an impression.

Your goal is to make people crave your posts, and to share them with their friends and peers. Post with purpose without being a fraud (we'll get more into that later in the **Diary**)!

Diary Entry #2

WHAT DO YOU WANT TO BE KNOWN FOR?

WHO DO YOU WANT TO SERVE?

WHY DO YOU WANT TO SERVE THEM?

WHAT BENEFIT WILL THEY RECEIVE FROM WORKING WITH YOU?

HOW DO YOU DELIVER THAT BENEFIT TO THEM?

Now. Define your brand in **one** sentence:

> *I help [the people who you want to serve] to [the benefit will they receive from working with you] through [how you can help them].*

The next time someone asks you what you do, you can confidently tell them in one sentence! For example:

> *I help [single moms] to [become debt-free] by [teaching them how to turn their ideas into physical products].*

Continue to play with it and over time you'll get it. You'll be firing off your one-sentence mission without thinking about it.

Step Three: Create your Instagram bio

Your bio is one of the most important features on Instagram. With so much competition, your bio is the best way to make a strong first impression. You only have three seconds to make that first impression, so you want to *kill it* at first glance!

Do you want them to join your tribe? Or do you want them to scroll right on past your page and, most likely, never visit again? Unfortunately, most IG pages are victims to the latter.

A good bio will stop someone in their tracks and make them say, "Wait. What? Who is this? I want to be her friend. I must follow her immediately."

The secret to creating great posts is to make people desire to learn more about you, to wish they were connected to you in real life, and to anticipate every post you create.

Like any good branding strategy, your bio won't speak to everyone. In fact, some people will read your bio and run for the hills. And that's a good thing. You want to attract people who like *you*. So be upfront about who you are and what your brand is all about.

You can read my bio on Instagram right here. Right now it says:

Some people will see that and be turned off right away. Who knows? Who cares? My bio is completely in line with my brand's voice and I only want to attract people who connect with my voice.

I tell people right off the bat what they can expect from me and you should do the same. I make it clear that I offer life-changing, inspirational content and I even share my own transformation: "Real teen mom turned millionaire mentor."

I also share my interests (business, beauty, family, and fashion) to attract my ideal tribe and provide a link for my followers so they can dig deeper into the ways I can help them. Your bio is the only place you can post live links. If you're not taking advantage of this feature, you're missing out on key opportunities to connect with your followers outside Instagram. Ultimately, you want a bio that gets people to take the next step.

So, in your next **IG Diary** entry, let's get that bio of yours together: Take a look at your bio.

- Is it engaging? Does it resonate with your ideal follower? Do you have a relatable bio picture?
- Do you position yourself as their solution?
- Are you using descriptive words that make people feel a certain way? Do you mention something unexpected that speaks to your brand?
- Do you have a call to action plus a link that leads people to take the next step with you? What step do you want them to take?

Use the brand sentence you created in the previous section to help you jumpstart your bio.

Step Four: Defining your visual style

One of the main goals of this book is to help you establish yourself as an influencer and recognizable brand, but having the perfect layout doesn't always convert to profits. I want to share with you what I've done to create a compelling brand without conforming to the cookie-cutter Instagram feeds we see all too often.

A lot of people are focused more on graphics and looking cool than getting conversions—and unfortunately for a lot of brands out there, the graphics are starting to look alike. Just because you have cool graphics and your page looks nice, it doesn't necessarily mean you are converting followers into customers. How do you know your page is converting?

When people are buying from you and swiping their credit card, you know your followers are converting. When your Direct Message inbox is full of people asking what they need to do to work with you—asking for the next steps—then you know your posts are converting.

As a marketer, your sole focus needs to be, "Why is my customer not buying from me?" or "What is going to make a customer buy from me?"

People are often more set on the layout of their page versus the conversion. For example, people that I coach personally with social media have 500 to 1,000 followers but their page is converting like crazy—they are making an extra two thousand to three thousand dollars a week on social media.

Then there is someone else with 50,000 followers and they have sent a message to my inbox saying, "Ronne I need to start a business…" and I'm like, "What? What are you talking about? You have this entire platform all these followers and you're not making *any* money at all?"

As you think about your brand, I want you to concentrate more on creative ways to convert your community into income than living some perfectly scripted life that looks cool but doesn't make you any money!

Diary Entry #3

WHAT ARE YOUR BRAND COLORS?

____

____

WHAT FONTS WILL YOU USE?

____

____

WHAT APPS WILL YOU NEED TO ALLOW YOUR PICTURES TO LOOK THE BEST?

____

____

IS YOUR INSTAGRAM PAGE IN ALIGNMENT WITH YOUR OVERALL BRAND?

____

____

WHAT TYPES OF IMAGES DOES YOUR IDEAL AUDIENCE RESPOND TO?

____

____

DO THEY MATCH YOUR BLOG, YOUR MARKETING MATERIALS, AND YOUR OTHER SOCIAL MEDIA CHANNELS?

____

____

Image is everything: How to build visual brand that goes viral

Now that we have built your undeniable visual brand on Instagram, let's talk about how to make your brand go viral! Pretty images and cute quotes can only take your brand so far. So what's the secret to growing a community of followers that like, share, and comment on your posts?

Engagement! But what is engagement exactly? Well, engagement is proof your following is organic. That it's real.

Have you ever come across a page that has 10,000 followers but when you take a closer look at their posts you see they only get two comments or thirty likes? This is a red flag and you can probably assume that this person bought their followers just to appear "popular"—but this is a big *no-no*!

Do *not* buy followers. Do *not* buy likes. Do *not* buy popularity. Real influence and engagement can't be bought! One good (and loyal) follower is worth a thousand fake followers.

One of my favorite quotes is, "The goal is not to look rich. It's to be rich in real life." Your goal is to build a real following, to have real people engaging with you, following you, and buying from you so you can actually be rich in real life!

Real engagement shows there is genuine interest in you and your brand. When people are commenting under your pictures, talking to you, responding to your captions, and you're talking back—this is what matters. It shows that your followers have a relationship with you. They are interested. That's really important because customers are not just attracted to brands specifically, they are attracted to someone they can have a real relationship with.

When you get to the point when you can say, "Hey girl! I hope you had a great weekend!" or "Your kids are beautiful!"—this is what real engagement looks like. So, remember, engagement is more credible than the following.

I can always tell when an account is not real or when an account has paid followers because you'll have thousands of likes and not one comment. Or you have thousands of followers and two likes. It just doesn't add up.

To make money on Instagram you have to convert and there's no place on earth where fake likes or fake followers turn into real profits!

Share "scroll-stopping" images

We all *love* liking and commenting on Instagram photos. I know I do. But for some reason, many business owners tend to throw up any old sad and boring photo that's easy to overlook or get lost in the feed. This is when "would-be" customers turn into social media ghosts.

When I initially got started, I owned a salon and used to take pictures of my salon employees doing hair, makeup, lashes, and things that showcased their talents. In an effort to grow my following, I began sharing results-driven pictures like before-and-after photos, customer testimonials, and behind-the-scenes snapshots of my day-to-day work. I allowed people to come into my world, and they were intrigued.

You see, to get the most out of Instagram, you must learn how to *slay* your images. Now before you panic, please know that you do not have to be a graphic designer or have a professional photographer in your back pocket. However, you do want to spend some time thinking about how you want to strategically style your images and invest time in finding the right apps that can enhance your photos.

If you're wondering what you should post? Here are a few ideas to get your creative juices going:

Fashion shots

If you love fashion as much as I do, Instagram should be one of your most frequently used apps. It's a great way to showcase your personal style and impress potential clients. Sharing a look of the day or look of the week (known as an OOTD for "outfit of the day" photo) is a great way to create styled shots that get a ton of engagement. Everybody loves a cute dress and a fly pair of heels, so if you like to play dress up, why not share your passion on Instagram?

Family + Lifestyle shots

Behind every brand is a person with family, friends, and a life outside of social media. I am a mom before anything else, and one of my goals is to help other moms like me build successful businesses from home. Family is a huge part of my success story. One of the reasons my Instagram page has been so successful is because I don't hide that. I share pictures of my kids. I share pictures of my husband, and I share pictures of me hanging out with my friends.

I believe that how you represent yourself and what your followers come to know about you matter. It reveals something about who you are and the kind of person they are following.

As a personal brand it is important to give people a glimpse into your daily life, your family's daily life and to show that you're human, just like them. It's through your lifestyle that people will ultimately feel connected.

Quotes

Everybody loves a good quote, and one of the most common types of posts you see on Instagram are inspirational quotes. I use picture quotes as a tool to boost engagement, motivate my community, and add visual variety to my Instagram feed. When used well, quote posts can generate tons of engagement, getting hundreds, even thousands, of likes and comments.

Quotes work well because people can easily relate to them but you must have a strategy behind how you use them. Don't just post the quotes you like. Post quotes that support the mission and purpose of your brand. That's why it's important to know your brand's purpose and the "why" of what you offer beyond just your products and services (which is what we took time figuring out in the previous lesson).

Once you know that, you can look for inspirational quotes that support that mission, helping you use picture quotes in a more targeted and focused way. Remember, you want your content to be aligned with your overall brand strategy.

P.S. *Do not*!! I repeat....*do not* flood your entire timeline just with quotes. That repels people, doesn't showcase your personality, and will not get much engagement if your entire wall is just full of quotes.

Do you need help creating gorgeous Instagram Quotes? Here are five apps you can try today:

- BeHappy.me
- Inspirably.com
- Textgram
- InstaQuote
- QuotesTags

Social trends + pop culture

Adding trends and talking about the latest news is a great way to increase engagement on your page. Why? Because in America people go about their day and no one asks them what they think. Many people want to give their opinion on so many things and social media, in general, is a great tool for starting conversations.

Since (nearly) everyone wants to give their opinion, posting about what's hot in the news is the perfect way to increase engagement on your page. People want to share what they think. Do it, use it, add it to your page, and I guarantee, when people can weigh in and share what they think, your engagement will explode.

You'll see people commenting, tagging their friends, and having healthy conversations on topics they care about. It will blow your mind.

Funny shots + memes

I know you're using Instagram to build your business and market your products but remember that your audience contains people that like to have fun too! When I post funny stuff on my page like grandmoms dancing or cute little dogs, people go crazy for it.

Apps: Snapchat

Snapchat has some pretty funny filters too, show people you have a sense of humor and that you're not all business all the time. Don't be too cool for school. People need a good laugh too!

Business tips

If you run a business, people aren't stopping by your feed just to see what cute cup you're drinking your chai tea latte out of, they are also looking for solutions. They want to be able to come to your feed and gain some perspective and insight on how to change their situation, solve a problem, or satisfy a need.

Use your IG feed to share your values as an expert and spotlight your knowledge in a specific area. You can also leverage your feed to inspire others on "getting started" or "staying in there" because you never know what people are going through or why they're scrolling on social media.

Product shots

Whether you have a physical product or a digital product, you have to share what you're selling if you want to make a sale. A beautifully placed product in your Instagram feed can really boost your sales. From videos to photos of you (or your customers) using the product, this is where a little creativity can go a long way.

While you want your feed to be a healthy mix of personal and business content, don't be afraid to share your products and services. If you lead with value, viewers will be eager to purchase the products and resources you recommend.

Create "customer-grabbing" content

This is a major component people miss about Instagram. A picture may be worth a thousand words but having content that people can relate to creates an engaged community of customers and followers. The key to attracting customers and going viral on Instagram is relatability.

Relate-a-what?

Yes! *Relatability* means that someone feels your life is similar to theirs. One of the reasons I've been able to have so much success on Instagram is because I can show my followers that I can be a huge goofball just as much as I can be a savvy, hardworking businesswoman.

My audience sees that I'm a mom, a friend, and a wife, but they also see me as a hard worker and committed leader as well. I believe they are excited to see the realness, the behind the scenes, but most importantly, they are excited about the transparency.

For example, if you're a mom running a business, there may be moms who follow you that have always dreamed of running a business. Your vibe will attract your tribe.

Instagram gives you the platform to reach those people, to inspire and encourage them to make their own business happen.

If you're a fashion blogger who loves showcasing your outfits, there is someone out there seeking to be inspired by how you put your clothes together. What will happen is the people who enjoy watching what you post will begin to follow you because you have some things in common. They're inspired by your posts and they're interested in following your journey. That is why it is so important to be relatable.

A lot of people want to hide the mess in their life, but the thing with me is that I am so straight up on Instagram. You're going to get the real me. A little rap music every now and then, and on Sunday you might get a little gospel! That's okay, because that's who I am. I'm not ashamed to let people know that when I'm working out, I need to get pumped, or that when I'm getting ready for a meeting I turn on a little hip-hop, and jam to a little Biggie Smalls!

Use custom hashtags

It's a great idea to use custom hashtags of your own to create spaces where pictures can be found that are associated only with your business.

Encouraging followers to use hashtags can be extremely beneficial. It allows you to see who is using your products or services while promoting your brand using Instagram hashtags that have a global reach! If your brand uses specific hashtags on Twitter or Facebook, use them on Instagram as well. Note: Take a picture of this book and put #RonneBTeachesIG so I can see who you are and connect with you!

Use trending hashtags

Another great way to increase your audience is to use any number of trending hashtags to join in a bigger part of the visual community.

Do you remember when Twitter's #followfriday seemed somewhat groundbreaking? Instagram users can leverage hashtags such as #ootd (outfit of the day) and #tbt (throwback Thursday) to drive awareness and visibility.

Prepping your posts

Once you've decided on the types of images and captions you want to share on Instagram, you will want to do a little bit of prep.

If you're shooting selfies, make sure the lighting is good and the image is not blurry. If you're shooting behind-the-scenes or product images, make sure your desk and home are clean and clutter-free. No one wants to see your laundry in the background, a crowded countertop in your bathroom, or dishes piling up in the sink!

When I coach social media professionals, I also tell them to make sure that they don't have stains on their carpets, make sure that their mirrors are not dirty, and make sure the dirty clothes hamper is not, you know, falling over behind them. Cleanliness is next to godliness!

I don't want you to feel like you have to have this perfect life. I am a Christian woman who loves Jesus that can still get down with a little hip-hop music at the same time. I am not picture perfect. I am a real, live human being who has managed to maintain a positive image while still dealing with life's obstacles. I believe this is what makes people relate to me. Don't be afraid to create content that shows your audience the lows with the highs and everything in between. Don't be afraid to let people into your world so they can get a glimpse into what you are really doing.

Just so you know, there are days you can take pictures when you're doing the laundry. There are days when I post pictures of me in my pajamas and a sweatshirt—when I'm not all glammed up.

Here's an example of a pic here:

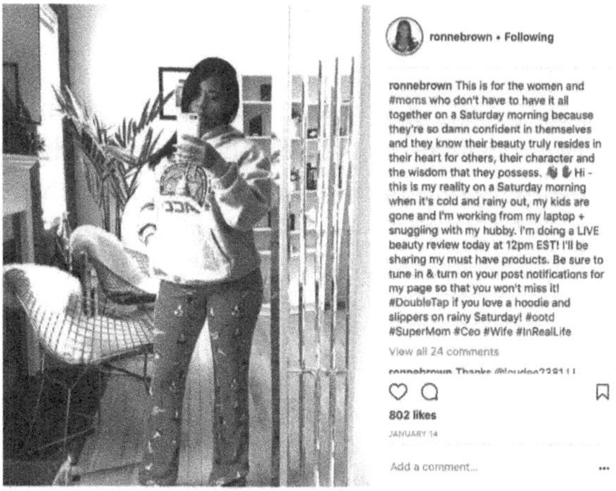

I am basically saying this post is for women and moms to know that you don't have to be glamorous on a Saturday, and that this is what my reality looks like when it's cold and raining outside, when I'm working from my laptop, and I'm spending time with my husband without the kids. Just look at the engagement: 802 likes, twenty-four comments. That post has so much engagement because while people want to see you dressed up, they also want to see the real life without the makeup and the dressed-up stuff. They want to see that you are a regular person just like them.

You don't have to hide. Be you! Relatability is so important! Now, if you need a little help improving your images here are a few of my favorite apps. Right now, I have an iPhone 7. Most smartphones give you the option to enhance your photos. You can increase the contrast, brighten the photo, and add different filters.

CAMERA 360

Has tons of filters and photo editing tools.

PHOTO GRID

With over 100 million fans, Photo Grid is the most popular Instagram collage maker. With Photo Grid, you can combine ordinary photos into photo collages worthy of sharing; you can decorate your pics by applying fantastic filters and by adding stickers and text.

SQUARE VIDEO

Never again will the 1:1 frame upload ratio restrict your ability to share your entire video. Square Video empowers you to capture and share your video within the ideal horizontal or vertical viewing ratio (16:9, 2:3…and so on). Simply load your content from your camera roll and Square Video will scale your clip to fit within the 1:1 frame, filling the gap with the appropriate letterbox.

Features include:

- Add a blur effect to fill your video or photo.
- Change the color of the letterboxes.
- Trim your video with the simple editing bar.
- Apply filters via the 'Effects' tab to your videos.
- Insert a clever caption and select from a wide selection of fonts.
- Select the perfect song to enhance your moment.

AFTERLIGHT ($1.39 FOR iOS, $0.99 FOR ANDROID)

With seventy-four filters, seventy-eight natural textures, 128 frames, and countless editing possibilities, Afterlight is the app of choice for many Instagrammers. Afterlight is one of the best (and most popular) apps out there. The shooting capabilities are excellent, along with the above average number of filters, frames, effects, and editing options.

When you're ready to post a new image to your feed, always think about what it looks like in relation to your overall brand.

Before I hit the upload button, here are some of the factors I consider first:

- Does the image match my overall brand theme and visual style?
- Does the image fit within my personal story, values, and beliefs?
- Is the light hitting what I'm snapping? Lighting is so important so make sure you're always hitting it from the front.
- Does the image look too busy, cluttered, or dark? I always make sure that when I'm taking my photos, they're clean and clear, bright, and visually attractive
- Does the image complement my caption and the text laid on top of the photo? Is it legible?

Hello hashtags

Or maybe, goodbye hashtags!! Contrary to what most Instagram gurus will tell you, when it comes down to hashtags, I'm not a big hashtagger. But what's a hashtag, anyway?

A hashtag is the pound sign (#) that is put in front of a word or phrase to make it searchable. When you search on Instagram including that hashtag, every picture that has ever been uploaded with that hashtag is curated in one spot. This is a great way to grow your network with people who you know have similar interests. Because people are using a lot of automatic commenting robots right now, you get all those corny people on your page who are like, "This is cool, nice shot...!" and all that type of stuff. They are not real people and the robots normally send a lot of spam to your page. I might do one or two hashtags here or there that are custom to my personal brand, but I don't have like 100 hashtags under my photos.

If you do decide to use hashtags, here are some tips to attract people who are interested in your brand.

Use location-based hashtags

If you have a location-based business, use hashtags relevant to your local community to connect with people in your area. For example, if you're a restaurant owner in Santa Monica, California, and your shop is on the pier, use the hashtags #santamonica, #pier, #losangeles, and #california, as these are relevant hashtags for your location and will attract a local audience who are more likely to search Instagram and other social media platforms using these keywords.

Scheduling your posts

Like most social media sites, posting content can be a real time-suck, and Instagram is no different. I get lots of questions on how much time you should spend building your Instagram community.

Well, I would definitely say one hour a day! It's really important to be active, to respond to comments, answer questions, explore other accounts in your niche, and reach out to potential collaborators, because building rapport is really important.

When time is tight, I also pre-schedule my posts. Most traditional tools like Hootsuite, Latergram, and Buffer don't allow you to fully automate your Instagram posts. You can pre-schedule them, but you still have to go in and press "publish" to post them.

Instagram also has an option where you can create a post then save it as a draft to post at a later time.

How do I save a post as a draft?

Once you start creating a post, you can save it as a draft and share it later:

1. Tap the box at the bottom of the screen, then take or upload a photo or video.
2. Add effects, filters, a caption, or your location.
3. Go back to the filtering and editing step, then tap the back arrow in the top left.
4. Select Save Draft at the bottom of the screen.

Note: If you don't edit the post, tag people, or add a caption or location, you won't be able to save the post as a draft. To see posts you've saved as a draft, tapand then tap Library. Posts will appear at the bottom of the screen below Drafts.

Recommended Tools for Scheduling Posts

Audience connection: How to engage your audience with conversations that convert

Picking the perfect image is just the beginning. It's how you engage with your audience once you've hit the publish button that really drives conversation and community. So how do you strategically and effectively grow your following once you've posted your pictures?

The 1-2-3 rule

A good way to activate and grow your audience is to follow the 1-2-3 rule. When you post 1 photo, comment on 2 and like 3. You're already on Instagram posting, so take a few moments to effectively boost your engagement at the same time.

Respond to comments

Don't be too cool to respond. If you're on social media to grow your business it's important to engage in activities that increase your conversion rates. Are you on Instagram to be popular or to produce profits? Hopefully, you're on it for the second reason and not the first.

Post quality content consistently

When it comes to posting on Instagram, I understand you don't want people to forget about you or your business, but instead of focusing on posting 24/7, I personally coach people to post three times a day to show the Instagram algorithms that you are an active user. This way your photos don't get lost in the feeds.

Some people post once a day. Others post several times a day. But above all, make each post special and meaningful.

Only people who engage with your photos will see your post, which is why engagement is really important. The people who engage with your photos are more likely to see your posts, whereas if you are posting things and people are not commenting, not engaging, or not liking your photos, people don't see them.

In order to stay on top of the Instagram algorithm and to make sure you are getting in front of your ideal customers, I always recommend you post at least three times a day: in the morning, the afternoon, and the evening. If you do this, you'll probably be able to catch your followers at some point throughout the day.

Ditch the salesman mentality

The biggest mistake people make is that they hop on Instagram and just sell, sell, sell, sell. No one wants to follow a sales page. People want to see you. People want to see your family. People want to see your fashion. People want to see you behind the scenes. They want to see your world!

You aren't following your favorite celebrity because you want to see what they are selling. You are following your favorite celebrity because you want a peek inside of their lives. Keep that in mind when it comes to marketing your products and services. No one is following you, so you can say "go buy this" on every single post. That's not attractive.

Your audience wants to see what you are wearing. They want to see how you get dressed. They want to see your covers rolled up on your bed sometimes. They want to see that you're a mom.

A lot of people follow me because I show that I'm a mother. I show that I coach a lot of people to success, but I also show people that I have a life, and it's not all about money and success. I have a husband and I have kids. People want to see that part of my life.

Mention people in your posts

Don't forget to mention the people in the photo or anyone you worked with to get the shot. Another great way to increase engagement and expand your visibility is to mention people who have relevance to your post. There may be times when you repost, or reference a photo from another brand or partner. Make sure you give credit where credit is due, or take time to mention them for his or her great work.

Tagged: @HHHGLUXE

Geotag your pics

I travel a lot and have been blessed to see many beautiful places. Are you on vacation? At a conference? Having a business meeting at a cool restaurant? Post it, then tag it! A great way to give people more insight into your fabulous lifestyle is to geotag your photos, which means to share the location of where you are.

The beautiful thing about Instagram is that even if you don't post right away from that location, you can share it long after you've left the area where you're geotagging.

Instagram will still pull up the location so you can share it after you've left.

(I will say, however, to do this with caution. As much as we love to share, we also want to take safety measures into consideration to protect ourselves.)

Chapter Sixteen:

Other Social Media

If you've already got a decent following on other social media platforms, capitalize on your community, by letting them know you're on Instagram as well. Make sure to add a link to your Instagram account on your website, Facebook Fan Page, and other sites you're currently active on.

To add your Instagram photos to your Facebook Fan Page, follow these steps:

First, locate and install the Facebook application. After you have logged into your Facebook account, make sure you have access to the fan page that you wish to merge with. Then, search "Instagram" using the search bar located at the top of the page. Select the "Instagram feed for your fan page" option under "Apps" from the drop-down menu of Instagram options that appears. Tap the blue button that reads "Go to App" to install the application.

Then, select the pages you want to add to Instagram. To do this, you'll have to give Instagram permission to connect to your pages. This page will show all the fan pages that the account can be connected to, but it won't automatically install Instagram on all of them (it's just an option.) To successfully allow access, you must click the blue button that says "Allow."

After allowing the Instagram application to access your accounts, remember to select all of the pages that you want to feature the Instagram feed. For example, if you only wanted to include Instagram on two of your Facebook pages, you simply click the blue button on those two indicating, "Add Instagram feed tab." This application will only allow you select one page at a time. If you want to add the Instagram feed to multiple fan pages, you must repeat the process for each fan page.

Linking your Instagram, Facebook, and Twitter accounts will allow you to share posts directly from Instagram to Facebook or Twitter. You can do this by tapping the settings icon in the top right-hand corner of your iPhone or Android and selecting the option that says "Linked Accounts." From there, you can choose either Facebook or Twitter and then enter the login information for that account.

After you have linked all of your preferred accounts, you can share a post to both Facebook and Twitter from the screen you use to you add a caption to the photo/video you're posting to Instagram.

Instagram also allows you to share content directly from Instagram to any Facebook Page you manage.

I personally feel that in business, when it comes to social media in particular, you can't focus on every platform. Whatever platform you focus the most energy on, the other one will lack. I recommend choosing two platforms that can easily tie into each other. I feel that using Facebook and Instagram is the perfect fit. (Not to mention Facebook owns Instagram now!)

Here's a prime example of how I cross-promote my social media content on both Facebook and Instagram:

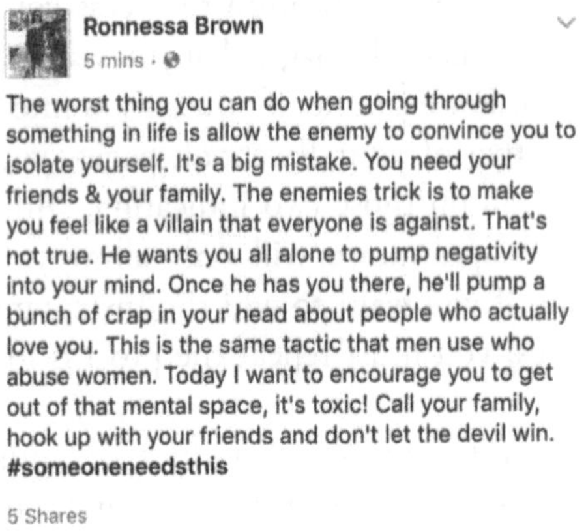

I simply took a screenshot of my Facebook post and shared it on Instagram. One piece of content, double the engagement!

When Instagram introduced live stories, I made a strategic decision to drop Periscope and Snapchat. I still do Snapchat a little bit because of all the filters, but I focus my energy on the platform that can give me the highest return on my time invested.

To ensure that you don't spend all day and night managing a million different platforms, over time you will discover how to get the most out of a platform by leveraging those that are mutually beneficial and work hand-in-hand like Instagram and Facebook.

Because I can post pictures, do live videos, live stories, and send virtual messages all on one platform, it just makes sense to utilize the platform that can offer the most.

When you're trying to juggle all things you become a jack-of-all-trades and a master of none. You want to work smarter, not harder, so simplify your life by narrowing down the amount of social media sites you try to use to grow your business.

Track what works

Analytics are important. They are simply a way for you to track and see how people are responding to your posts, the posts that are getting the best feedback, along with the best times to post, based on your audience's response.

When using Instagram for business, it is important to do your research, know your numbers, and stay on top of your stats so you know what works best to maximize growth. If you upgrade your Instagram account into a business account, you will be able to take a look at the analytics. It will show you how many followers you have, how many new followers you got in one week, how many people follow your page, how many impressions you've gotten on each photo, and how many people actually clicked on a picture. It will also show you what time your followers are online the most.

The tools are there. Instagram gives you everything you need to grow your business—you just have to pay attention.

Popularity versus Profitability

Speaking of stats, when it comes to building a business online it's easy to get caught up in the number of followers, likes, and comments you get. But let's get real for a moment...

DO YOU WANT TO BE POPULAR OR DO YOU WANT TO BE PROFITABLE?

False celebrity is not going to do you any good if you can't find a way to turn your gifts into profits. As you continue to build your business, I want you to do it with purpose. Lead by example, serve your community, and be the type of person people want to follow.

When people book you for an event, the person they meet and sit down with when the cameras aren't rolling needs to be the same person they see on Instagram.

My ultimate goal is to help people find solutions. I don't want to be popular, I want to be profitable. That's what is important to me and it's what should be the most important to you too.

Diary Entry #4:

Choose the primary social media platforms you want to use along with Instagram.

SOCIAL MEDIA SOURCE #1:

SOCIAL MEDIA SOURCE #2:

HOW WILL YOU TRACK YOUR ANALYTICS AND MEASURE YOUR RESULTS?

Share real life stories that showcase your products

With more than 600 million monthly active users and more than ninety million daily uploaded photos and videos, Instagram Stories is becoming one of the best ways to showcase your brand and products.

On Instagram, the key is to give people a taste of what goes on in your daily life. Sharing your content through stories and video is one of the most effective ways to get personal with your audience.

There are so few marketers that create real transparent content. With Instagram stories and video you can create content that is uniquely you, that shows the best of "you." What you put on Instagram should be an expression of yourself and your vision; the most popular accounts on Instagram use video and stories to communicate that vision in real time!

Instagram video

With Instagram video, you can record short video clips ranging from three to sixty seconds long. Ready to record a video? To upload a video from your library or to record a new one, first tap the plus symbol at the bottom center of the screen.

To upload an existing video from your phone's library, select "Library" at the bottom of the screen, select the video you would like to share, add filters or trim the video, type a caption for your content, and click share.

To record a new video clip, select "Video" at the bottom of the screen. Select and hold the circle to begin recording. To stop recording before you reach the maximum time capacity, simply lift your finger. Otherwise, the recording will continue until you've reached its maximum capacity.

You can either film a continuous video or you can piece together several mini clips, which enables you to be creative. To create multiple mini clips, begin recording and lift your finger off of the record button to pause between videos. To add to the clip, press and hold the record button and repeat this until you're done capturing your video footage. At any point, you can delete a clip by pressing the delete arrow just below the record button.

The current maximum video length is sixty seconds. Again, after you've recorded or uploaded a new video, you have the option of adding a filter, a caption, and your location prior to sharing.

If creating a live video is too much pressure, you can pull an existing video from your phone's gallery. IPhone users can upload multiple saved videos, splicing them together, and there are also a number of video apps you can use for more advanced video editing and uploading.

Here are three of the best video and editing apps for Instagram:

VSCO CAM (FREE FOR IOS AND FREE FOR ANDROID)

This is the go-to app for many brand builders. VSCO Cam is an easy-to-use editing app that allows you not only to take photos with a built-in, high-quality camera, but also edit your masterpieces with filters and editing tools.

DSCO (FREE FOR IOS)

If your regular Instagram content is feeling a little boring, it might be time to try something new. Adding GIFs to your Instagram content strategy is shown to increase engagement and conversions. Creating a GIF might seem intimidating, but the DSCO app (by VSCO) makes it quick, easy, and fun. You can capture, edit, and share your GIF directly to Instagram through the app. You can also add it to Tumblr, Twitter, and Facebook.

CLIPS VIDEO EDITOR (FREE FOR IOS)

If you're looking for the simplest way to edit your videos for Instagram, this app is billed as "the simplest video editor in the world." With Clips, you can add music, dissolving transitions, speed up or slow down your video, add text slides, add voiceovers, split clips, edit for square or landscape export, and share to Instagram, Facebook, Facebook Messenger, and text message.

Everybody is living in a microwave world, and nowadays people want good content fast. Video is replacing reading so when you are doing videos, you want to make sure you're getting straight to the point, because people's attention spans are getting shorter and shorter.

For me personally, I don't think I would want to watch a video right now that's more than half an hour, on the long end. Preferably if I can get it all under five minutes, that would be great. If I could get it under one minute, that would be even better. Keep it informative, short and sweet, and to the point. In addition, make sure you are shooting videos because you can also see what people like by how many people view them. You build off what people are engaging and what they are leaning towards according to the views. Not sure what to say? Start with this:

> *"Hey, this is [your name]. In this video I am going to share [list what you'll share]." Move into your key points and then close with, "If you want to learn more, connect with me at [how people can reach you or call to action]."*

I shot a video that was boring and I wasn't talking about much of anything, but then I shot a different video where I gave five tips to grow your business in five days. The boring video of me just sitting around my house, where people could see my home in the background, got more engagement, with 200 views, than the other video with the business tips, which only got fifty views. That lets me know people want to see more of my personal life.

That will give me the idea that I can talk about business, but maybe I should do it where people can get a little background of my home at the same time. You are able to monitor what people want to see according to the analytics. That's why I love Instagram right now! The analytics will definitely change the game while providing insight on what's a hit versus what you may want to avoid.

Instagram stories

We've talked a lot about how important it is to be relatable as an entrepreneur and not just focus on a logo or tagline. Instagram stories are so powerful, because they allow you to share authentic moments that give your audience a glimpse into who you really are.

Creating Instagram stories

Stories are temporary videos or photos that are strung together to form a slideshow gallery that, well, tells a story. So how do you use Instagram stories to grow your business? Let's break down the steps to launching your first Instagram story.

While on the home page, tap the circular profile image with the plus sign to begin.

- By swiping from left to right at the very bottom of the screen (beneath the round button), you'll discover that you have the option of a normal picture, live recording, boomerang, superzoom, and stop-motion, just to name a few.
- You can take a photo by tapping the round button, or you can record a video by pressing and holding the round button for up to ten seconds.
- To turn on the flash, touch the thunderbolt icon, and to switch the camera back-and-forth, just touch the arrows.
- If you want to use filters or animation, touch the icon in the bottom, far right-hand corner.

If you would like to upload an existing image or video from your camera roll, you can do so by clicking the image icon in the bottom far left-hand corner.

- If you'd like to make it fun and doodle on your image, you can select one of the three pen types, add an emoji using your keyboard, or you can even swipe right to select any of the featured filters.

- When you're done, tap "Send To" and select "Your Story" to share. You can also send the content as a direct message to specific recipients.
- Your Instagram story will appear at the top of your friends' news feed and on your profile page for up to twenty-four hours when users tap your profile picture. You have the option of saving, deleting, and sharing your live story by opening it, tapping "More" in the bottom right-hand corner, and selecting any of the options listed.
- You can monitor who saw your story by simply swiping up when viewing the photo or video.

If you realize there is someone who is seeing your Instagram story that shouldn't be, just tap the "X" next to their username to block them from your stories.

You can keep your story private by selecting the "Settings" icon in the upper right-hand corner of your profile and choosing to hide your story from select users. You can also restrict a user's ability to reply to your messages.

If you have an active audience base on Instagram, you should jump on stories right now. You have the opportunity to increase your engagement and increase your visibility. Remember on Instagram, there are hashtags, geotags, and the Discover section that will help increase your chances of being found!

Are you ready to do your first Instagram story?

Diary Entry #5

CREATE YOUR FIRST INSTAGRAM STORY WITHIN THE NEXT 24 HOURS! THINK OF THREE MOMENTS YOU CAN SHARE ON INSTAGRAM STORIES:

1. ______________________________
2. ______________________________
3. ______________________________

Testimonials

People want real proof that what you're pitching works! Testimonials, before-and-after photos, and video praise are all great ways to show that your products, your services, your brand can get results.

People want results—period!

Selfies are not the only pictures that make a statement. Whether you sell physical products, digital products, or services, every time someone buys something, uses one of your products, or has something amazing to say about you or your brand, capture it in a picture or video.

Never pass up an opportunity to capture photos with your students, customers, clients, and peers. It's a great way to share the experiences with your audience, while capturing an instant endorsement from a happy customer or business partner.

Diary Entry #6

DO YOU HAVE ANY TESTIMONIALS YOU CAN SHARE ON YOUR PAGE?

____

____

____

CREATE A FOLDER ON YOUR DESKTOP OR IN YOUR PHOTOS APP WHERE YOU CAN KEEP SCREENSHOTS AND IMAGES THAT ENDORSE YOU AND YOUR BUSINESS.

Yield massive profits with community-building collaborations

Collaboration is the new competition! What better way to build your brand than to have an influencer promote you, your business, or your products?

Instagram is the breeding ground for influencers and a great place to hook up with other brand builders who can bring value to your business. Now let me be clear, you want to make sure you are connecting with people who can add the same value to your business as you do theirs.

When seeking collaborations, you want to reach out to people who are able to bring something to the table as well. This means if you're coming to me with 1,000 followers, and you want to share each other's pages, but I have 100,000 followers, it's not worth it for me because I'm helping you but you're not helping me. The return is not worth the effort.

But if we each share the same following or have the same range of followers, then we can work together. I can give a shout-out to you, and you can give a shout-out to me. I can promote your company, business, or brand, and you can promote my company, business, or brand, and it is beneficial for both of us.

The reason collaboration is amazing is because the goal is to build both parties platform!

When you can expand your audience by leveraging other people's platforms, it's like list sharing with the ability to grow a massive following on social media, because now those people are on your list. When you are putting another business or brand in front of your following, you're exposing your list to that brand. That type of value is called "influence." When *you* have influence, there's no way you should be exposing your followers to other people's platforms for free, when people can and should pay you for that exposure.

That's called marketing.

Your community is not just a bunch of people who like and comment on your posts. Your community is an invaluable asset that will allow you to expand your brand. If you're prepared to put in the time and commitment, you can easily find yourself in a position where you can start making serious money from your Instagram account.

Are you unsure what to do?

Chapter Seventeen:

Affiliate Marketing

With affiliate marketing, you can promote a product for a company or individual and get paid per sale. Instagram allows you to market and highlight other peoples' products using photo or video and drive sales through your affiliate's URL. This link will be provided by your affiliate, but it can only be used in your bio, not in the caption of a photo.

If you sell products or offer a service, you can use your Instagram feed to up your marketing potential. Posting beautiful images of a product or service can attract clients, customers, and potential business partners.

One way to utilize Instagram to market your brand is posting videos or images from "behind the scenes" of your daily operations. Capture attractive images of the hard work and intimate details that go into building your brand. For example, you can feature pictures of a gourmet cuisine as it's being prepared for a private catering event, action shots and captivating images of your team setting up a venue for a wedding or social event, or images of you working out in the gym with clients. People like to see work as it progresses. Encourage your customers to share images of your products and make sure you re-post them. The "Repost for Instagram" app is a quick, secure, and easy way to re-post your customers' photos.

Sponsored content is another way to earn additional money. On Instagram, popular brands with engaged followers can create original posts highlighting a specific product or service from another supported brand. A sponsored post is generally a photo or video and includes product- or service-specific captions that may include branded hashtags or @mentions.

Tap Influence can be useful for brands that are searching for opportunities to connect influencers to specific sponsored content. You have the ability to create a profile that describes your brand as well as the type of content that you create, the type of brands that interest you, and the type of brands that may be interested in your products and services. Brands will contact you if they are interested in your profile.

Ifluenz is another marketing platform used by influencers on Instagram. It's also a platform where both brands and influencers can come together in an effort to monetize and promote one another.

If you ever decide you no longer want to manage your popular Instagram account (with a preferred following of 40k or more), and it has a concentrated niche, you can actually sell your account. Sites such as "Fame Swap" and "Viral Accounts" are sites that offer the sale and purchase of social media influencer accounts.

Who you follow matters!

A lot of entrepreneurs aren't really familiar with how social media works, specifically Instagram. When you're following certain businesses and personal brands, you're actually promoting them. So, I don't follow people who are not adding value to my business or brands in which I am not genuinely interested. I also don't follow people who are promoting or posting things that are unprofessional or don't represent my brand in a positive light.

Why?

Because when people click that "Follow" button on your page, Instagram automatically recommends or suggests about three to four other accounts for you to follow. You're literally advertising for those people. Once you follow someone on Instagram, you're telling Instagram and the social media community that this person, this brand, this business has *my* endorsement.

People can see if you're following someone who doesn't align with your brand and believe me, it doesn't look right. It also matters who you follow, because when you're online and liking pictures, it also shows up in your activity. People who follow you on Instagram can see the photos that you're liking every single day. If what you are liking, commenting on, following, and endorsing doesn't align with your brand, it has the potential to turn your ideal customer off!

Tips on how to follow the right people & where to find them

You may find the Instagram interface a little tricky to use at first but with the right directions, it's easy to find and "follow" new and old friends on Instagram in a number of ways.

Here's how:

How can I find and follow people that I know?

I can help you find and follow your current Facebook friends, and contacts in your phone or tablet who are already registered on Instagram. (These instructions are for both iPhone and Android users.)

On your profile, tap settings in the top right-hand corner. Select "Facebook Friends" and all of your Facebook Friends will appear. You can select "Follow All" or you can individually select which Facebook Friends you want to follow. You can follow these same steps to connect your Instagram to your Contacts list by selecting "Connect Contacts" in the settings menu.

How do I find people I might want to follow?

At the bottom of your main screen, tap the "Search & Explore" icon which is where you will see and be able to search for photos, videos, and people that you may be interested in following.

Explore this section to see posts that may peak your interest from accounts that you're not already following. Use the search bar at the top of the screen to search for specific people, hashtags, locations, and events. Type what you're looking for in the search bar and then hit search to find photos you might like.

You can also find people you might like to follow by searching for followers of people you already follow. Click on the Instagram profile of someone you already follow and tap the drop-down arrow next to the "Following" button. Then,

Instagram will give you suggestions and you can follow people that interest you.

What happens when I connect to my contact list?

After you choose to connect Instagram with your contact list on your phone or tablet, you'll be able to see which of your contacts are on Instagram, regardless of their activity. You can select who you want to follow from the suggested list. Your contact list is regularly synced while it's connected. Your contacts are securely stored and can be disconnected at any time.

Diary Entry #7

Take some time to purge your unprofessional friends. Unfollow any brand or business that is not in alignment with your brand vision and mission.

Search for on-brand influencers to follow and begin engaging with their posts. If you see opportunities for collaborations, reach out to those influencers to see how you can work together in a way that benefits the both of you.

INFLUENCER #1

____

INFLUENCER #2

____

INFLUENCER #3

____

INFLUENCER #4

____

INFLUENCER #5

____

Is it too late to build your Instagram following? Absolutely not!

Remember, I started with zero followers just like you. We all start from nothing and we build. The key is to find something that will set you apart and offer real value to your audience. Be authentic to who you are. There are so many people on social media who have looked at other people's pages, tried to mimic them, and as a result, left their own personal flavor out of it because they are looking to be like someone else.

Apply the tools. I meet so many people who read books that inspire them, or empower them, or get them motivated. The purpose behind this book is not to leave you hyped, pumped up, and feeling like you can conquer the world—it's to get you to a place where you *apply the tools*. You take action and you conquer the world. That's the biggest thing for me, getting people to take action. So, take the tools that I've given you and start using them immediately.

Right now, go back on your Instagram page and look at the people who have commented, or find some new people on social media and say hi, or compliment them, or make conversation. I dare you to start building some relationships today.

Your authenticity is so important when it comes to your page because people need to see the value you can give and they need to see who you are. When you're pretending to be someone else, you're losing that relatability, which is the most important piece to seeing results on Instagram. Be you! Everyone else is taken!

Living Paycheck-to-Paycheck Is Not Living

I became an entrepreneur in 2010 and have been a full-time entrepreneur since 2012. I am a single and divorced mom of five. I lead a big team in a direct sales company. Prior to running that business, I was an executive assistant and I also owned my own cleaning company.

Before working in the direct sales business, I was living paycheck-to-paycheck. Considering that I have five children, it was really hard for me to provide for everyone. My full-time job was my sole source of income and my cleaning business was just breaking even after expenses. I had never successfully broken a consistent and stable profit. I was looking for a different way to earn where I could see some tangible extra income coming into our house.

Emotionally I was a wreck. It is stressful enough just living, period, paying bills, juggling expenses, raising children, managing a household, just trying to be an adult, right? I had so much on my plate: Mom, employee, business owner, household manager. It was exhausting. No matter what I did, it never seemed to be enough. I was juggling basic needs but there was no room left for my desires and dreams. It was stressful for me. I felt like I was not a good mom because I was so stressed out. I was constantly rushing to get to a job and didn't always have the time to be the parent I needed to be with them. I commuted a total of three and a half hours every single day between dropping kids off at daycare and getting to work by a certain time every single morning. I was in my twenties and it was just tough. My kids had no additional opportunities to excel. They weren't allowed to be a part of any extracurricular activities because I couldn't afford any and because it was not an option either for my husband or myself to pick them up early or take them to extracurricular activities. Most nights, I didn't get home until almost 8:00 p.m. I was in a toxic marriage at that time, which also caused extreme stress. I stayed longer in the marriage for financial reasons. Of course, when I thought about leaving, I thought the little bit of help that he did provide would be gone. I was looking for an exit route. And naturally, I needed that exit route to be something positive.

When I started my business a couple of things happened. Number one, I made more income than I ever thought I would. It happened really fast and that finally provided me with a way out of my marriage. Number two, it gave me the confidence to leave and raise my kids without my husband. After being with someone for so long, I didn't really know if I could do it on my own. Once I saw that I could build something so massive while still working a full-time job, while still in a toxic relationship, while still being a mom of five, while still under an enormous amount of stress, I realized my true capability.

Making more income gave me options. Something I didn't have access to working a full-time job were options. I made however much someone else told me I had to make. I had to work whatever hours they told me I had to work in order to provide. When I was making money on my own terms it allowed options and those options allowed me freedom. When I stopped living paycheck-to-paycheck, I was less stressed and became the person I always knew I was inside. One of the things I noticed most was how much my children changed once I did not live paycheck-to-paycheck because my patience level changed. I could spend more time with them. When I didn't have to stress over having to tell my kids "no" all the time, when having money created more time for me, and more opportunity for my kids, that's when I knew I had hit the jackpot.

I see now that I was a prisoner to my stress, to my bills, to my marriage, and to my negative emotions. Money is not everything, but we need it. Try saying that money is not everything to a person who doesn't have enough money to always cover their bills. Making more money gave me access to a whole new life and new way of being powerful in the world.

Leaving My Dead-End Life

My cleaning business earned enough to meet expenses but earned no profit. I was a one-man show and sometimes if I had several home bookings over the weekend, I would have to pay someone to help me. I was also paying for my initial costs like gas to commute and the products that I used to clean the home. After factoring in all those expenses, there was barely anything left. I was lucky if I could pay a utility bill, maybe my cellphone bill. And that just wasn't enough. At a bare minimum, I needed to be clearing at least one thousand additional dollars per month, and I was not. I was also spending more time out of the home and away from our children.

Ronne and I have been friends since 2008. Ronne also used to have a cleaning business and I met her through mutual friends on social media. When I found out Ronne had had a cleaning business, I called her. We ended up becoming friends. I had no business savvy at all. I was looking to start my own business, but I wasn't sure how to come up with pricing or where to start. Ronne gave my first tips and pointed me in the right direction.

Although I've now dissolved the cleaning company, I've made some lasting relationships that carried over into my direct sales business. Ronne introduced me to the direct sales business. I had no experience in this either. The only reason I said "yes" is because I trusted Ronne. Once I got in, almost immediately she said something to me that just clicked in my head that changed how I run my business, even today. She said, "Just simply share your story." Until then, in my everyday life I didn't really share myself. Once I began to share my story, my business blew up. It allowed people an inside glimpse into my life.

Ronne was a strong mentor who helped me to be successful in business. She was more than just a pretty face posting selfies online. She was a real person and I could relate to her. Ronne herself has successfully exited out of a long-term relationship that was not great for her prior to her current marriage. She always encouraged me that she would support me no matter what, and she poured into me that I was so much more valuable than I realized.

Here is my advice to you: First, find your tribe. Find women who are dealing with similar situations. In my case, it was running a cleaning business, believing in myself, and exiting a long-term relationship with some grace and dignity. If you have kids, find your people because they will understand what you're going through.

My life now is totally different. For the last five years, I have owned my time. Where I was living paycheck-to-paycheck, now my oldest daughter is in college. I don't know how I would have afforded this before. Because of these opportunities I pay her cash for her college and she stays on campus which is expensive and not something I would have been able to do five years ago. It is rewarding. Working with Ronne has changed the entire legacy of my family.

The flame inside you is enough to ignite an entire forest. Because Ronne was brave enough to let her light shine, it lit a light inside of me, which in turn lit a light inside my children. And we go around and light other people up. We give them the hope to believe they can overcome challenges not feel ashamed if they are struggling, dream bigger. There is light at the end of the tunnel if you are brave enough to walk to it.

My biggest realization on this journey is that we are more powerful than what we are.

Get yourself a Ronne Brown. Everything I learned from Ronne is found in these pages. You have access to Ronne Brown just like I did; all you have to do now is take action. There are truly no limits except the ones you place on yourself. As creative as you can become about your vision, you have the power to truly go for it. Most people don't get to where they're going because they don't take any action. They allow their thoughts to get in the way. Do not be afraid to fail. Just go for it. The first step is to take the first step and do not overthink it. Now it's your time.

—Kimberly Scott, Entrepreneur

CONCLUSION

By now you probably understand why I am such a huge fan of Instagram. Instagram is the real deal, and if you have not started building your brand and marketing your products on Instagram you are missing a huge opportunity to boost your bottom line.

We live in a visual world where image is everything and Instagram lets you be a part of it. Instagram is not only beautiful, it also helps you strengthen your relationships in a fun way.

The beauty of this platform is that Instagram gives business owners and entrepreneurs the power to get creative with marketing and promotion of their business. It gives them the power to connect with their audience, to create a sense of community that they would never be able to achieve offline.

If you are planning to take your Instagram account to the next level, be sure to follow and implement the strategies of the big players. You don't have to be a big brand to make a big impact on Instagram, but you do have to know how to play the game.

Remember, it's not about sell, sell, sell. Keep your content balanced by promoting not only your products and services but your personality and creativity as well. Success on

Instagram is all about engagement with your followers and creating a healthy combination of promotion and play.

Marketing is now a visual medium driven by photos and videos. Whether being consumed through desktops, smartphones, or tablets, visual marketing is driving consumer engagement and Instagram is smack dab in the middle. There is no shortage of online tools and resources to make marketing on Instagram profitable and the opportunities to build a successful business online are limitless.

Learning how to strategically integrate Instagram into your overall marketing plan and finding new ways to reach and influence your target audience will position you well above the competition.

Creating an engaged community is crucial to home-based business owners and entrepreneurs. After all, our followers are who make our lives possible! They become our biggest fans, clients, and friends.

ACKNOWLEDGMENTS

To my family, thank you for being by my side while I embark on this crazy journey to conquer all the things I want to do.

To my mom, thank you for sticking by my side and encouraging me through every trial in my life. And for sending me money to put food on the table, when you barely had it to give.

To my dad, for always making me feel like I was special when I was a little girl, for showing me love, and boosting my confidence. For teaching me how to fight and stand up for myself. It trickled down to every area of my life. You taught me how to be fearless.

ABOUT THE AUTHOR

Ronne Brown is a wife, mother, coach, author, speaker, entrepreneur, and overcomer. She has influenced thousands of entrepreneurs by teaching them to achieve success on their own terms. Hailing from Washington, D.C., Brown inspires others to live and dream big.

Ronne worked hard to change the trajectory of her life. She went from being a statistic to a success story. She worked long hours as a janitor while she was pregnant, but she didn't allow that obstacle to make her lose sight of her purpose. Even though the odds were stacked against her, she was determined not to allow her past circumstances stop her from achieving her goals. After being laid off from her job with only an unemployment check as her income and three children to take care of, she knew she had to make a change. She was determined to face her fears and step into her purpose. The lessons she learned on her journey as a teen mom gave her the courage to launch several business ventures.

In 2009, she founded High Heels High Goals, an exclusive, nonprofit organization that teaches women how to be successful entrepreneurs and empowers women to reach their goals. Because Ronne has a heart for women, on any given day you can find her pouring into the lives of other women by speaking positive words, sowing seeds to assist with start-up costs in a new business venture, or coaching a woman to success.

In 2014, Ronne launched The Millionaire's Academy, where she teaches people all over the world how to leverage the direct sales industry and earn income from home. Through this program, she has helped men and women create six-figure incomes, become debt-free, and live life on their own terms. Her vision is to empower others to succeed in business and inspire people to leave a legacy for generations to come. She coaches entrepreneurs by using the strategies and methods she used to grow her own business and develop as a leader. She believes, "Success is no accident. If you want to achieve amazing things and build a successful business, you have to do it on purpose for a purpose."

Because of her discipline, hard work, and dedication, she was able to turn a minimum-wage income into a seven-figure salary within a few short years. She achieved this goal without any formal training or business education. Ronne is the face of success. Instead of focusing on fear, pain, and the difficult days, she decided to endure and focus on the promise.

When Ronne is not coaching other women, leading seminars, writing, or speaking, she enjoys spending time with her husband and her four children.